Low-Cost, Low-Tech Innovation

Like much of the research on small and medium-sized enterprises (SMEs), innovation studies of small enterprises have commenced later and are less numerous. The focus of such studies remains high-technology enterprises, which continue to attract both academic and popular interest, oblivious to the innovative endeavours of people in traditional low-tech industries.

This book attempts to address this imbalance through a comprehensive analysis of innovation in this largely neglected area. Based on case studies of seven small innovative food companies, this book presents an in-depth analysis of innovation in the Scottish food and drinks industry and unravels a lesser-known approach to effective low-cost product innovation, which is simple and economical, yet elegant and successful.

Using careful data collection and rigorous statistical testing, the analysis and findings in this book address a wide spectrum of interests: academics in business schools, policy makers in governments and executives and entrepreneurs in food and other low-technology sectors.

Vijay Vyas is Senior Lecturer in Enterprise and Entrepreneurship and Course Director of MSc, Innovation Management and Entrepreneurship at Portsmouth Business School, a former visiting Professor at Lancaster University Management School and a former Professor of Business Economics at the MS University of Baroda in India. He is a founding member of the Society of Entrepreneurship Educators (a group of entrepreneurship academics in premier business and technology schools in India) and is the founder of the current Global Entrepreneurship Monitor (GEM) team in India and was a member of the team between 2012 and 2014.

RIOT! Routledge Studies in Innovation, Organization and Technology

Low-Cost, Low-Tech Innovation

New product development in the food industry

Vijay Vyas

Routledge
Taylor & Francis Group

LONDON AND NEW YORK

First published 2015
by Routledge
2 Park Square, Milton Park, Abingdon, Oxon OX14 4RN

Simultaneously published in the USA and Canada

by Routledge
711 Third Avenue, New York, NY 10017

*Routledge is an imprint of the Taylor & Francis Group,
an informa business*

British Library Cataloguing in Publication Data
A catalogue record for this book is available from the British Library

Library of Congress Cataloging-in-Publication Data
Vyas, V. S.
    Low-cost, low-tech innovation : new product development in the
food industry / Vijay Vyas.
        pages cm
    Includes bibliographical references and index.
    1. Food industry and trade.   2. Technological innovations.
3. New products.   I. Title.
    HD9000.5.V85 2014
    664.0068′5—dc23
    2014021064

ISBN: 978-0-415-81899-5 (hbk)
ISBN: 978-0-203-57707-3 (ebk)

Typeset in Sabon
by ApexCovantage, LLC

To my wife Renuka, my daughter Shruti
and my son Kushan

Contents

Figures

Tables

Acknowledgements

I am grateful to Professor Ron Masson, Mrs Susan Laing, Mr Aidan Craig and Dr Janice McMillan of Edinburgh Napier University for their help, advice and support during the research on which, this book is based. The help from Professor Ron Masson, Mrs Susan Laing, and Mr Aidan Craig was particularly significant in conducting the interviews of the key people in the case study companies. Edinburgh Napier University is acknowledged gratefully for the resources and support provided to me during the course of research on which this book is based.

I am also obliged to the Managing Directors of seven Scottish food SMEs who allowed me to carry out the case studies of their enterprises, and the 'contact persons' in 85 Scottish companies, who responded to my survey.

Professor Jonathan Michie of University of Oxford is acknowledged gratefully for sending me his unpublished paper 'Cooperation and Innovation: Evidence from the Community Innovation Survey', co-authored with Marion Frenz and Christine Oughton and for his permission to cite it and Mr Robin Pollok, a Director of Food Initiative Ltd for pretesting both the paper and online versions of my survey questionnaire.

Bloomsbury Publishing Plc is acknowledged for permission to use updated material from my paper 'Relationship Between R&D and Innovation: Implications for Scottish Innovation Strategy', published as Chapter 5 (pp. 82–96) in their book *Sustainability and Development: Paradigm Shift in Knowledge Creation and Innovation*.

Professor Gioia Pescetto, Dean of Portsmouth Business School and Professor Paul Trott, Head of the subject-group Strategy, Innovation and Enterprise at Portsmouth Business School, are gratefully acknowledged for their help in providing me time to write this book.

Preface

The history of study and analysis of innovation goes back to three quarters of a century. Much of the early work on innovation, however, concerned the large corporation and analysed innovation from a high-technology perspective. Innovation studies of smaller enterprises commenced later and were less numerous. The focus of such studies, however, remained high-technology firms, ostensibly, the quintessential unit of small-business innovation. This bias was perhaps due to the drama and theatre reflected in the acts of such enterprises. The breakthrough nature of their innovations, the scorching pace of their growth and the demolition of some of the revered names in the world business by them romanticised many of the more visibly successful of these ventures and made them a part of folklore of business history as well as a focus of academic and journalist interest. In contrast, innovative endeavours of people in traditional low-tech industries did not evoke similar response. In absences of their ability to usher in 'breathtaking' innovations, they grew rather slowly and did not confront large corporations head-on, knowing full well the disastrous consequence of such a contest. Academics and media ignored these 'lacklustre' enterprises. This book, to address the imbalance, attempts a comprehensive analysis of innovation in this hitherto largely neglected area of inquiry.

This work, however, is prompted not only by a relative scarcity of work on innovation in small low-tech enterprises. It springs from the belief that innovation studies of such enterprises are equally, if not more, essential. Though small firms' roles in, income generation and employment creation is generally well appreciated, it is less understood that even in the developed economies the competitiveness and rates of growth are influenced substantially by the functioning of low-tech and traditional industries. The recent research shows that firms in low-tech and medium-tech industries are actively involved in innovation and contribute more to economic growth than what the firms in high-tech sectors do, even in the developed countries, and the perception that high-tech sectors are the sources of productivity, employment and output growth in the developed economies is not supported by the empirical evidence. The economic future of the developed countries and the well-being of their people, thus, depends significantly on the performance of these industries. Given the contribution of innovation in the competitiveness and growth of businesses, the need for studies of innovation in traditional low-tech industries – such as the one attempted here – is therefore too obvious to be stressed.

Vijay Vyas
Portsmouth, UK
Monday, 7 July 2014

1 Innovation and new product development in the food industry
An overview of international research

Food and drinks, one of the largest industries in the world, has been regis-tering a sustained 'recession proof' growth over last several decades. This industry, valued at $5.7 trillion in 2008 and expected to be worth $7 trillion in 2014, like most other major manufacturing and processing sectors, is dominated by enterprises principally from Europe and the USA. However, China and India are gradually emerging as major potential contributors to this sector (IMAP, 2010).

Constant growth in this industry is due largely to a long-term trend of rising global incomes and population but also, in no small measure, to con-tinuous introduction of new products and processes. There has also been a long tradition of research on innovation and new product development in this industry. Unsurprisingly, the bulk of this research involves investigation of North American and European enterprises, along with occasional studies emanating from Australia and New Zealand. From Asia, studies on the Thai food and drinks industry have recently been more regular, whereas studies investigating African and Latin American food companies are rare.

This overview of the last 4 decades of research on innovation in the food and drinks sector looks at findings of a range of studies investigating both the process of innovation as well as the factors influencing innovation suc-cess. Much of this work is exploratory, and some studies happen to be the first and/or the only study of innovation in the food and allied sectors in the geographical region in which they are conducted. There is a remark-ably high level of constancy in the findings of these studies, revealing a significantly unchanging pattern of innovation and new product develop-ment in this industry, reflected both in the process details and in determinant identification.

The approach to innovation in this sector seems to be marked by a high level of conservatism, and despite the epoch-making events of technological change that have transformed the process of new product development in many other industries, food and drinks enterprises have largely continued to develop new products using almost the same process reported by Nys-trom & Edvardsson (1982) in one of the earliest studies involving 20 major Swedish food processing companies for the 1969–1978 period. Though there are signs that some of the enterprises are bucking this trend and breaking new ground, not too many enterprises have taken uncharted routes and, more importantly, those that have done so have not achieved any spectacular success to tempt others to follow suit. The reason for such conservatism is not difficult to decipher. As the following analysis shows, those who have developed new products not very different from their existing products are invariably the most successful new product developers in this industry.

Historically, the food and drinks industry has consistently exhibited a low research intensity, reflected in much lower R&D-to-sales ratio in comparison to other industrial sectors (Sandven & Smith, 1993 and Galizzi & Venturini, 1996). Jones (1995), in his survey of 120 food and drinks firms from around the world, found that only 10% have an R&D facility. In Nigeria, Ilori, Oke & Sanni (2000)found few companies investing in formal R&D whereas Capitanio *et al.* (2009) reported that only 28% of 234 investigated Italian food and drinks manufacturing firms carry out R&D. Food companies seem to avoid the high costs of R&D, widely perceived within the industry to be 'unnecessary' for innovation success, particularly the smaller food companies which happen to dominate this industry in numbers. When Martinez & Briz (2000) reported 'lack/scarcity of appropriate sources of finance' along with 'excessive perceived risks' of innovation as the main barriers to innovation, it is obvious that they are referring here to R&D-led innovation, which not too many food and drinks enterprises seem to practice.

There is significant evidence that the largely non-R&D food and drinks product development is singularly focused on incremental innovation. Koku's (1998) content analysis of 284 news items published in the *Wall Street Journal* between 1980 and 1989 on new product announcements found incremental innovation as the dominant form of food sector NPD. Ernst & Young (1999) reported that only .04% of new products introduced in the Spanish food industry in 1997 could be rated as truly new. Martinez & Briz's (2000) study, based on two successive surveys – first of 149 Spanish food companies and then of 54 innovative food companies amongst them – also found that innovative activities of companies in this sector are predominantly incremental. Bogue & Ritson (2006), using descriptive sensory analysis by the experts as well as hedonical evaluation by untrained end users of Irish food products, concluded that successful product innovation invariably involves incremental rather than radical change. Similarly, Bhaskaran (2006), based on a survey of 87 Australian seafood SMEs, concluded that incremental innovation offers substantial competitive advantages to SMEs. Although there are not many studies which elaborate on the precise nature of this incremental innovation, van der Valk & Wynstra's (2005) refer to relevant trends that food companies should focus on when deciding to successfully vary their existing products, such as changing lifestyles, increasing interest in convenience foods, growing incomes and the consequent expectation of higher product quality. Most importantly, despite a popular perception, this search for incremental variation has not proceeded in any substantial way towards the development of health foods. The unanticipated failure of low-fat variants to deliver the promised premiums to their creators is caused by food consumers' conservative and dogged attitudes, resulting in the battle between taste and the perceived health benefits, going in favour of the former (Bogue & Ritson, 2006). Though the industry experts have been maintaining for some time that low-fat foods promise significant potential in years to come (Longman, 2001), research on the subject does not show that the food companies are anywhere near realising this yet.

Shunning R&D and being satisfied with only an incremental change, however, is not the behaviour of the very largest of food and drinks giants. They do not seem to worry too much about the high costs of cutting-edge science and are willing to invest in a search for radical new products. They do not, however, succeed consistently in these efforts, and the successful amongst them are few. Alfranca *et al.*(2004), from a close scrutiny of nearly 17 thousand patents granted in the US between 1977 and 1994 to 103 of the largest food and drinks MNCs in the world, found that very rarely an enterprise exhibits an innovative spell lasting more than 4 years, and a small number of persistent patentees account for nearly 80% of the all patents granted to the agri-food sector MNCs. With such a record of the big boys in this industry, it is not a wonder that shunning R&D makes a lot of sense to smaller players with shallow pockets.

The reason for a focus on incremental innovation, avoidance of 'unnecessary' high R&D budgets and low research intensity in this sector is also analysed by the researchers in this field. They attribute it essentially to the fact that food habits take a long time to change. Food consumers have historically shown and continue to show a remarkable conservatism, and people around the world are very reluctant to eat products on a regular basis that are very different from what they are used to eating. This poses an almost insurmountable challenge to a product developer who would like to develop a radically new food product. Nystrom & Edvardsson (1982) explained that consumers' unwillingness to try completely new products means that only the enterprises that develop new products which are variants of their existing products achieve significant commercial success. In Jones's (1995) study, respondents defined the very term *innovation* as 'modification of existing products'. Galizzi & Venturini (1996) also support the observation that consumers in general are conservative in their food choices and find it difficult to accept radically new food products. One of their related finding is a weak relationship between R&D intensity and innovation. Prospects of achieving commercial success through incremental innovation that does not necessitate investment in R&D along with inability of R&D to lead to innovation with some certainty explain a historical reliance on incremental innovation and avoidance of R&D investments in this industry. Despite a continued evidence of positive engagement of food SMEs with innovative activities (Baregheh *et al.*, 2012), the nature of innovation in this sector thus has not undergone any significant change.

Another major finding emerging from these studies is significant and growing retailer involvement in new product development in this industry, which Hughes (1997) has been amongst the first to report. Citing Hoban (1998), Parr *et al.* (2001), Knox *et al.* (2001) and their own unpublished work, Stewart-Knox & Mitchell (2003), in their analysis of NPD in food companies in the UK, USA and Denmark, identify deep involvement of retailers as a vital success factor in innovation in this sector. Fortuin & Omta (2009), from their study of nine food processing MNCs in the Netherlands, also report this, and so does Colurcio *et al.* (2012), based on their study of five Italian and six Swiss food SMEs. This working together of retailers and small food companies in new product development ensures that the innovation in this sector is neither purely market-led nor it is purely production-led (Hughes, 1997). However, though the retailer involvement is widely seen as beneficial to small food companies trying to develop new products, the retailer motives of this involvement and its consequences for small food companies are complex. Retailer's interest in encouraging and abetting small food companies to develop new food products is generally focused on creating products for the high end of value chain, and their objective in this is to compete with major food brands. This cocreation, however, is not a partnership between equals, and the retailers enjoy a distinct bargaining advantage (Hingley & Hollingsworth, 2003). There is also an element of coercion as retailers practically force food companies to either innovate, or lose shelf space to the competitors (van der Valk & Wynstra's, 2005). However, it is also found that when a small food company networks with a large retailer for the purpose of innovation, the resultant conflict helps them maintain 'the competitive driving force and creativity' (Colurcio *et al.*, 2012).

Despite an apparent high probability of NPD success while cocreating with a large retailer and assured shelf presence at multiple outlets, the new product failure is still significant in this industry. Redmond (1995), based on a range of previously published industry survey data, found new product failure rates in the food and drinks industry much higher than in any other industry. Looking at the issue from an ecological perspective, he concluded that a major contributing factor in this is 'competitive overcrowding'. The food and drinks market is saturated by existing products as well as swamped by new product introductions. Rudolph (1995) similarly reported that during 1993, 80% to 90% of more than 8,000 new food products introduced in the American retail market failed in less than a year. Low costs of ushering in incremental change and a sense of security provided by large retailer involvement seem to make too many small companies attempt to innovate too often. Unusually high new-product failure rates thus appear to be the consequence of a creative profligacy fed by complacence due to retailer involvement and low costs, and consequent low risks of failure. Interestingly, despite strong evidence of retailer involvement leading to product innovation success, van der Valk & Wynstra's (2005), in their study of Dutch and Scandinavian food companies, do not find any conclusive evidence of *supplier* involvement in new product development success in the food and drinks industry.

Another significant finding is the focus in this industry on product rather than process innovation. The reason for this is not difficult to fathom. Process innovation, which has high capital cost (Jones, 1995), does not fit well with low-cost, low-risk, low-tech models of innovation prevalent in this industry. However, that these enterprises can make substantial gains by embracing process innovation that entails higher risks is obvious. Galizzi & Venturini (1996) found that amongst Spanish food and drinks companies the percentage of highly innovative firms, those that earn more than 50% of the sales from process innovation, is twice of what is earned via product innovation.

Cross-functional cooperation within the enterprise is another hallmark of the innovation process in this industry. Suwannaporn & Speece (2000), in their study of new product development by five MNCs as well as 10 Thai and two Taiwanese large companies, found participation by and cooperation amongst functional specialists a strong predictor of new product development success. Their later investigation of 114 Thai medium-to-large food companies also found the same (Suwannaporn & Speece, 2003); so does a survey of 93 Thai food companies, nearly half of which are SMEs, by Dhamvithee *et al.* (2005). This gives an indication that cross-functional cooperation's role in new product development success cuts across firm size. Inclusion of Thai as well as Taiwanese firms in the first cited study and a similar finding by Capitanio *et al.* (2009), based on data from a study of 234 Italian firms on the positive role of quality of communication between R&D and marketing in innovation success, suggest some validity to these finding across regions. In a study, from a different perspective, Munksgaard & Freytag (2011) found that enhanced internal collaboration and improved cross-functional communication in turn is aided by complementor involvement (a company's complementors are the firms whose activities increase the value of its outputs).

Firm size has consistently shown to be a determinant of innovation in this industry. Avermaete *et al.* (2003), based on an investigation of 55 small Belgian food companies, found the size (though not the age) of the enterprise influencing its ability to innovate. Dhamvithee *et al.* (2005), based on a survey of 93 Thai food companies of all sizes, found firm size to be a significant determinant of new product development success. Huq & Toyama (2006), based on a sample survey of 62 firms in the Thai food industry, found only firm size to be a statistically significant determinant of technological capability for new product development. However, Capitanio *et al.* (2009), based on data on 234 firms extracted from the survey of Italian manufacturing firms for 2001–2003, did not find a relationship between firm size and R&D expenses. This, though, does not invalidate the general evidence of the impact of firm size on innovation in this industry because, as stated earlier, R&D investments in of itself are insignificant in the food and drinks sector, and the relationship between R&D and innovation is weak in this industry.

Jones (1995), in his survey of 120 firms from a range of countries, found that small companies do not go for formal business analysis as a part of their NPD efforts, and the idea-generation phase of NPD in particular is informal. Bogue (2001), based on the study of 25 Irish food companies, reported a mix of formal and informal approaches to new product development, which he describes as 'essentially a stage gate approach with fewer gates and fewer stages'. Ilori *et al.* (2000) also found innovative Nigerian food companies going through fewer NPD phases identified in literature.

A focus on creating variants of their existing products and low or nil R&D investments, however, means that companies do not develop capabilities to exploit technological opportunities. Muscio *et al.* (2010), in their study of 87 Italian food SMEs, identified 287 customer problems requiring a solution. The investigated firms, however, had no wherewithal of technological solutions to these problems that could enable them to translate latent demand into real demand. Martinez & Briz (2000) observed the dominant role of demand pull rather than technology push innovation in this industry. This, though, is not an exclusive attribute of the food and drinks industry. In their study of 252 new products in 123 Canadian industrial manufacturing companies, Cooper & Kleinschmidt (1986) found that the majority of successful ideas are market-driven, while only a few are technology-driven.

The other determinants of innovation in the food and drinks industry reported in the literature include the involvement of top management in product development (Ilori *et al.*, 2000); strong market orientation (Bogue, 2001); market and consumer knowledge (Stewart-Knox & Mitchell, 2003); environmental scanning (Ngamkroeckjoti *et al.* (2005); outsourcing of activities (Spaulding & Woods, 2006); regional networking (Gellynck *et al.*, 2007 and Karantininis *et al.*, 2010); quality of human capital (Fortuin & Omta, 2009); relevant knowledge and relationships (Spena & Colurcio, 2010); efforts of the regional public research institutes (Arias-Aranda & Romerosa-Martínez, 2010); vertical integration and export orientation (Karantininis *et al.*, 2010); flexibility and ability to respond quickly to changing customer tastes and preferences as well as emphasis on quality (Bogue, 2001).

As stated above, evidence of ground-breaking innovation in this industry are rare. One study by Broring *et al.*(2006), involving 54 Canadian nutraceutical R&D projects, reveals that even in this radical new field, some enterprises still rely on the use of existing innovation processes for front-end decision-making. Though there are enterprises that are willing to leave the trodden path, to do so they rely upon partners to fill in gaps already recognised at the front-end of exploration. Often the enterprises that use their existing processes are consumer-focused and their quest largely market-driven, whereas enterprises that break new ground and are dependent on other partners to forge ahead are involved in a search that is technology-driven. A majority of enterprises fall in the former category, a finding also reported by Cooper & Kleinschmidt (1986) as well as by Kohlbecker (1997).

References

Alfranca, Oscar, Rama, Ruth and Tunzelmann, Nicholas von (2004) Innovation spells in the multinational agri-food sector, *Technovation*, 13(6):343–73

Arias-Aranda, Daniel and Romerosa-Martínez, M. Mercedes (2010) Innovation in the functional foods industry in a peripheral region of the European Union: Andalusia (Spain), *Food Policy*, 35(3):240–46

Avermaete, Tessa, Viaene, Jacques, Morgan, Eleanor J, Crawford, Nick (2003) Determinants of innovation in small food firms, *European Journal of Innovation Management*, 6(1):8–17

Baregheh, Anahita, Rowley, Jennifer, Sambrook, Sally and Davies, Daffyd (2012) Innovation in food sector SMEs, *Journal of Small Business and Enterprise Development*, 19(2):300–21

Bhaskaran, Suku (2006) Incremental innovation and business performance: Small and medium-size food enterprises in a concentrated industry environment, *Journal of Small Business Management*, 44(1):64–80

Bogue Joe (2001) New product development and the Irish Food sector: A qualitative study of activities and processes, *Irish Journal of Management*, 22(1):171–91

Bogue, Joe and Ritson, Christopher (2006) Integrating consumer information with the new product development process: The development of lighter dairy products, *International Journal of Consumer Studies*, 30(1):44–54

Broring, Stefanie, Cloutier, L Martin and Leke, Jens (2006) The front end of innovation in an era of industry convergence: evidence from nutraceuticals and functional foods, *R&D Management*, 36(5):487–98

Capitanio, Fabian, Coppola, Adele and Pascucci, Stefano (2009) Indications for drivers of innovation in the food sector, *British Food Journal*, 111(8):820–38

Colurcio, Maria, Wolf, Patricia, Kocher, Pierre-Yves and Russo Spena, Tiziana Russo (2012) Asymmetric relationships in networked food innovation processes, *British Food Journal*, 114(5):702–27

Cooper, R G and Kleinschmidt, E G (1986) An investigation into the new product process: Steps, deficiencies and impact. *Journal of Product Innovation Management* 3(2):71–85

Dhamvithee, Pisit, Shankar, Bhavani, Jangchud, Anuvat and Wuttijumnong, Phaisarn (2005) New product development in Thai agro-industry: Explaining the rates of innovation and success in innovation, *International Food and Agribusiness Management Review*, 8(3):1–17

Ernst & Young (1999) *New Product Introduction, Successful Innovation/Failure: A Fragile Boundary*, Paris: Ernst & Young Global Client Consulting

Fortuin, Frances T J M and Omta, S W F (Onno) (2009) Innovation drivers and barriers in food processing, *British Food Journal*, 111(8):839–51

Galizzi, G and Venturini, L (1996) *Economics of Innovation: The Case of Food Industry*, Heidelberg: Physica-Verlag

Gellynck, X, Vermeire, B and Viaene, J (2007) Innovation in food firms: Contribution of regional networks within the international business context, *Entrepreneurship & Regional Development*, 19(3):209–26

Hingley, M and Hollingsworth, A (2003) Competitiveness and power relationships: Where now for the UK food supply chain? Proceedings, the 19th Annual IMP Conference, Lugano, Switzerland

Hoban, Thomas J (1998) Food industry innovation: Efficient consumer response, *Agribusiness*, 14(3):235–45

Hughes, Alex (1997) The changing organization of new product development for retailers' private labels: A UK-US comparison, *Agribusiness*, 13(2):169–84

Huq M and Toyama M (2006) An analysis of factors influencing the development of new products in the Thai food industry, *International Journal of Technology Management and Sustainable Development*, 5(2):159–72

Ilori, M O, Oke J S and Sanni S A (2000) Management of new product development in selected food companies in Nigeria, *Technovation*, 20(6):333–42

IMAP (2010) Food and Beverage Industry Global Report-2010, www.imap.com/imap/media/resources/IMAP_Food_Beverage_Report_WEB_AD6498A02CAF4.pdf, accessed on 12/08/2014

Jones, Peter (1995) Developing new products and services in flight catering, *International Journal of Contemporary Hospitality Management*, 7(2):24–28

Karantininis, K, Sauer, J and Furtan, W H (2010) Innovation and integration in the agri-food industry, *Food Policy*, 35(2): 112–12

Knox, B., Parr, H., & Bunting, B. (2001) Model of 'best practice' for the food industry, Proceedings of the British Nutrition Society, June 20–22, University of Ulster, Coleraine, Northern Ireland.

Kohlbecker, S (1997) *Forderung Betrieblicher Innovationsprozesse–Eine empirische Erfolgsanalyse*, Wiesbaden: German University Publishing

Koku, Paul Sergius (1998) Innovation and information management in the food industry, *British Food Journal*, 100(6):278–85

Longman, B (2001) *Future Innovations in Food 2001: Forward-Focused NPD and Maximizing Brand Value*, London: Reuters Business Insight

Martinez, Garcia Marian and Briz, Julian (2000) Innovation in the Spanish food and drinks industry, *International Food and Agribusiness Management Review*, 3(2):155–76

Munksgaard, Kristin B and Freytag, Per V (2011) Complementor involvement in product development, *Journal of Business & Industrial Marketing*, 26(4):286–298

Muscio, Alessandro, Nardone, Gianluca and Dottore, Antonio (2010) Understanding demand for innovation in the food industry, *Measuring Business Excellence*, 14(4):35–48

Ngamkroeckjoti, Chittipa, Speece, Mark and Dimmitt, Nicholas J (2005) Environmental scanning in Thai food SMEs: The impact of technology strategy and technology turbulence, *British Food Journal*, 107(5):285–305

Nystrom, Harry and Edvardsson, Bo (1982) Product innovation in food processing – a Swedish Survey, *R&D Management*, 12(2):67–72

Parr H, Knox B & Hamilton J (2001) Problems and pitfalls in the reduced fat food product development process, *Food Industry Journal* 4(1):50–60

Redmond, William H (1995) An ecological perspective on new product failure: The effects of competitive overcrowding, *Journal of Product Innovation Management*, 12(3):200–13

Rudolph, M (1995) The food production development process, *British Food Journal*, 97(3):3–11

Sandven, T and Smith, K (1993) *Innovation Activities and Industrial Structure: Industry and R&D in a Comparative Context, European Innovation Monitoring System, EIMS Publication, 1,* Luxembourg: European Commission, Directorate General XIII

Spaulding, Aslıhan D and Woods, Timothy A (2006) An analysis of the relationship between supply-chain management practices and new product development time: A case of the North American confectionery manufacturers, *Journal of Food Distribution Research*, 37(2):1–11

Spena, Russo Tiziana and Colurcio, Maria (2010) A cognitive-relational view of innovation in the agri-food industry: The fresh-cut business, *International Journal of Innovation Management*, 14(2):307–29

Stewart-Knox, Barbara and Mitchell, Peter (2003) What separates the winners from the losers in new food product development? *Trends in Food Science & Technology*, 14(1):58–64

Suwannaporn, Prisana and Speece, Mark, (2000) Continuous learning process in new product development in the Thai food-processing industry, *British Food Journal*, 102(8):598–614

Suwannaporn, Prisana and Speece, Mark (2003) Marketing research and new product development success in Thai food processing, *Agribusiness*, 19(2):169–88

van der Valk, Wendy and Wynstra, Finn (2005) Supplier involvement in new product development in the food industry, *Industrial Marketing Management*, 34(7): 681–94

2 Business innovation

Meaning, antecedents, process and consequences

Research over the last 50 years has consistently linked innovation with business success. Innovation is shown as a major contributory factor in the growth of firms (Mansfield, 1968, 1971); new products and processes, the fastest growing product groups, or 'clusters' (Freeman, 1974); the rise and dominance of large corporations ascribed to the use of new technology (Temin, 1979); better business performance related to the higher measures of innovation (Cavanagh & Clifford, 1983); levels of competitiveness linked with the levels of innovativeness (Dosi, 1988); firms using innovation to differentiate their products from competitors are *twice* as profitable (Pavitt, 1991); innovation as a key element of business success (Nonaka & Takeuchi, 1995); high-growth companies receiving a higher percentage of sales from new products relative to competitors (O'Gorman, 1997); innovating firms displaying lower probability of stagnant or declining employment in comparison to noninnovating firms (Frenz *et al.*, 2003); innovative businesses growing more than noninnovative businesses (European Commission, 2004) and firm innovativeness positively influencing both its financial position as well as its value (Rubera & Kirca, 2012).

Definition of innovation

Dictionary definitions of *innovation* usually focus on the development and successive refinement of inventions into usable products or techniques that are deemed worthy of being launched in a market or used internally within an enterprise (Frenz & Oughton, 2005). Amongst scholars, however, there is a fair amount of noticeable disagreement on the definition of innovation. This is attributed to the heterogeneity of sources and outcomes of innovation, which makes it difficult to identify and analyse it (Dosi, 1988) and is partly responsible for often-conflicting outcomes of research on innovation (Le Bars *et al.*, 1998 and Grunert *et al.*, 1997).

As inventions and innovations are associated phenomena, innovation scholars make it a point to clarify the distinction between the two. It is explained that although invention is a prerequisite for many innovations, it is only when an invention is exploited commercially that it results in an innovation (Brenner, 1990). Another, though less popular, approach to distinguish innovations from inventions has been to claim that inventions relate to new ideas in general, whereas innovations are ideas that are new within a specific context (Van de Ven *et al.*, 1989; Damanpour & Evan, 1984 and Damanpour, 1987).

From yet another perspective, a distinction is made between innovation and R&D, where R&D is shown to be concerned with the commitment of resources to research and the refinement of ideas aimed at the development of commercially viable products and processes, whereas innovation is concerned with subsequent product (or service) development processes. From this perspective, the following linear model of the process of innovation is visualised:

Research → Development → Innovation.

Innovation, however, is considered a nebulous concept. Godin (2003) believed that the ambiguity in meaning is caused by the following factors:

1 Depending on the analyst's research focus and convenience of data availability, it is defined as an *outcome* or an *action*.
2 There is no settled opinion on whether an innovation should be new to the world, to the nation, to the industry or to the firm.
3 With reference to process innovation, a firm can be innovative both by inventing new production processes and by using new technologies invented by others.
4 Conducting R&D as well as acquiring advanced technologies and employing highly skilled workforces all are perceived as being innovative.

Factors 2 and 3 in the abovementioned list are not really significant, as the taxonomy of innovation described later in this chapter clarifies these issues. The precarious link between R&D and innovation, however, is indeed not understood adequately, and its consequences in Scotland, in the shape of a flawed government policy, are discussed in some detail in Chapter 5. The more important point, however, is that the seeming ambiguity in the meaning of innovation is superficial, and as will be explained later in this chapter, it is possible to accommodate all notions of innovation within a unifying concept of *innovation span*.

The earliest definitions of innovation are credited to Joseph Schumpeter (1934), who arguably is the most influential early writer on entrepreneurship and innovation, and their pivotal role in the process of economic change. He includes five manifestations of innovation in its definition:

1 Creation of new products or qualitative improvements in existing products
2 Use of a new industrial processes

3   New market openings
4   Developing of new raw-material sources or other new inputs
5   New forms of industrial organisations.

The influence of the Schumpeterian vision of innovation persists to this day and can be seen in the European Commission's Green Paper (1995:1) on innovation that defines it as

> renewal and enlargement of a range of products and services and the associated markets, the establishment of new methods of production, supply and distribution, the introduction of changes in management, work organisation and the working conditions and skills of the workforce,

and in Edquist's (2001) summary description of innovations as new creations of economic significance normally carried out by firms (or sometimes by individuals).

OECD (1981, p. 15), however, takes a more restricted view of innovation and limits it only to new product and/or process development efforts, though it has a more comprehensive vision of *product*, in which it also includes *social services*. It defines innovation as "the transformation of an idea into a new or improved saleable product or operational process in industry and commerce or into a new approach to a social service".

The Oslo Manual (OECD, 1997:39), on which Europe-wide Community Innovation Surveys are based, limits its view of innovation to technological products and processes (TPP), which are defined as "all those scientific, technological, organisational, financial and commercial steps, including investment in new knowledge, which actually, or are intended to, lead to the implementation of technologically new or improved products or processes". For the purpose of measurement, it considers a firm innovative "if it produces one or more technologically new or significantly improved products or processes in a three-year period".

Some analysts also emphasise the beneficial effects of innovation. In one such view, innovation is described as the "intentional introduction and application within a role, group or organisation of ideas, processes, products or procedures new to the relevant unit of adoption designed significantly to benefit the individual, the group, the organisation or wider society" (West & Farr, 1990:9).

Taxonomy of innovation

A parallel and overlapping effort to define innovation is to construct a taxonomy of innovations, as seen in Figure 2.1. The creation of such a taxonomy is considered necessary and important, as disaggregation is crucial for progress with regard to identifying the determinants of innovation (Edquist, 2001). The following types of innovation emerge from this effort.

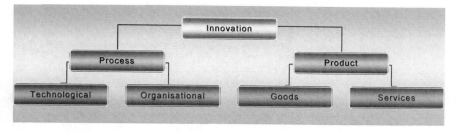

Figure 2.1 Edquist's taxonomy of innovation
Source: Edquist, 2001

Technical versus organisational innovation

A very common taxonomical effort has been to differentiate between technical and organisational innovation (Daft, 1978). *Technical innovation* refers to development of new products, services and production processes (Daft, 1978; Damanpour & Evan, 1984 and Knight, 1967). *Organisational innovation,* on the other hand, refers to innovations that are related to alteration in an organisation's structural and administrative procedures (Daft, 1978; Kimberly & Evanisko, 1981 and Knight, 1967). Adam Smith's (1776) analysis of the division of labour is an early example of organisational innovation and the study of its impact on productivity. In the food industry context, the most relevant organisational innovations are those that relate to logistics and supply-chain management.

Product versus process innovation

Product innovation deals with the production of new products and services to create new markets or to satisfy current customers. Process innovation is reflected in the improvements or introduction of new production technology (Knight, 1967 and Utterback, 1971).

Radical versus incremental innovation

Radical innovation represents a completely new product or process and incremental innovation a significant improvement in an existing product or process. Radical innovations have the power to result in substantial and rapid transformation of production whereas the effects of incremental innovation are felt more slowly, though their cumulative impact may be just as significant (Frenz & Oughton, 2005). Radical innovation brings about a nonroutine change to the very core on how activities are carried out, while incremental innovation is usually part of routine changes that do not deviate much from present organisational activities (Dewar & Dutton, 1986 and Ettlie *et al.,* 1984).

New to the firm versus new to the market innovations

This refers to the diffusion of the innovation from innovator to imitators. It is understood that most of the benefits from innovation arise from the diffusion of the innovation rather than its introduction (Vyas, 2005), and the full economic benefits from research are only realised after the processes of invention, innovation and diffusion are complete (Hollander, 1965). The economic effects of innovation are strongly influenced by the speed of its adoption by follower firms and/or consumers (Frenz & Oughton, 2005), which in turn is determined by network effects, the costs of adopting the new technology, the availability of finance, investment in fixed capital, proximity, cooperation between firms, market size and structure as well as institutional, social and cultural factors (Hall, 2005).

Determinants of innovation: Internal characteristics of enterprise

A significant part of innovation literature is focused on identifying the determinants of innovation. The internal factors found to be significantly related to the innovative performance of firms are presented in Figure 2.2 and explained in detail subsequently.

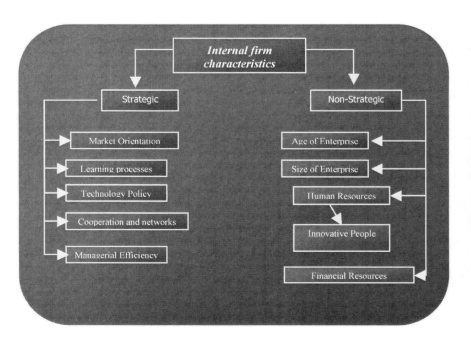

Figure 2.2 Internal determinants of innovation

Internal strategic factors

The organisation and processes internal to a firm are considered the most influential in determining its innovative performance. If at a point in time and space some businesses are more innovative than others, then they must have something internally distinctive to explain the difference. This notion has a strong intuitive appeal, and an impressive array of studies have explored and tried to vindicate it, making it by far the most pursued innovation research theme. The determinants of innovation that emerge from this pursuit can be listed as follows.

Market orientation

Understanding and anticipating customer needs and quickly and efficiently incorporating them in new products has been a recurrent conclusion of analysis of large firm innovation. It is shown, for example, that providing significant value to the customer is positively related to successful new products and negatively related to failures (Zirger & Maidique, 1990); firms that are able to reach the market earlier and efficiently with products that meet the needs and aspirations of customers gain considerable competitive advantage (Wheelwright & Clark 1992); the successful products meet customer needs better than competitive products and reduce the customer's total costs, providing high value-in-use (Cooper & Kleinschmidt, 1993); when product innovators do not learn about customer needs, they often end up developing products that are seriously flawed (Dougherty & Heller, 1994 and Hopkins, 2001); relative product quality, value-for-money and greater end-user benefits have significant roles in the financial performance of new products (Montoya-Weiss & Calantone, 1994) and product superiority – defined by the customer – is the most important aspect of a successful product development project (Cooper & Kleinschmidt, 2000).

Scholars trying to ascertain whether the insights gained by researching large business innovation have validity for SMEs have found that in terms of market orientation, successful SME innovators are no different from successful large firm innovators. In an analysis of 150 Greek SMEs, Salavou *et al.* (2004), for instance, identified market orientation as one of the strategic determinants that improve SMEs innovative performance. Lindman (2002) used a similar measure of market orientation to gauge the innovative efficiency of SMEs in the Finnish metal industry. Lewrick *et al.* (2011:48) found that "strong competitor orientation, a key ingredient of market orientation, has positive relationship to incremental innovation for start-up companies".

Heydebreck (1997) showed that the integration of customers into the product innovation processes leads to a higher degree of success in achieving company objectives. In the success of small high-tech firms, the role of market orientation and effective strategy formulation is often stressed (Oakey & Cooper, 1991, Roberts, 1991 and Dodgson & Rothwell, 1991). The crucial aspects of a heightened market orientation in these studies include competition analysis, cooperation, partnerships, speed and flexibility, among others (Soderquist *et al.*, 1997). Lindman, (2002) listed the ability to explore and reach potential markets, fit between the market needs and the firm's resources, product planning from the inception, targeting the international market, span of market experience, pioneering attitude and the understanding of customer needs and user circumstances amongst the factors that mark the state of a firm's market orientation.

Learning processes

Innovation involves the creation of new products and processes. It thus needs a set of skills and orientation different from one that is sufficient for rote manufacturing and depends crucially on the quality of an organisation's learning ability. Organisational learning, in turn, depends on how the knowledge formation process works and drives the innovation strategically in an organisation (Stata, 1989). It fosters creativeness and the ability to spot opportunities for innovation (Angle, 1989). It is applicable to both process and product innovation (McKee, 1992). Learning orientation is an indication of an appreciation of and need for absorbing new ideas (Hurley & Hult, 1998). Organisational innovation is dependent on learning (Mezias & Glynn, 1993) and is related to the firm's knowledge base (Cohen & Levinthal, 1990). Continuous learning is a way to attain and expand competitive advantage (Morgan *et al.*, 1998).

Technology policy

Technological change is at the heart of innovation. It is true that organisations involved in innovation sometimes get the signals from the market on what kinds of products to develop; how to create them is, invariably, a technological issue. An organisation's ability to answer the question 'how can the technology at its command be deployed to create a product to cater to an emerging or hitherto unfulfilled need' is a measure of the state of its technology policy (Vyas, 2005:113). Ettlie & Bridges (1982:3) explained that "(the technology policy) involves such things as recruiting technical personnel, committing funds to new technology development and building or maintaining a tradition of being at the forefront of a technological area in a particular industry". Soderquist *et al.* (1997) quoted several empirical studies relating to a firm's innovative performance with the existence of a well-developed technology policy and claimed that the presence of an explicit policy to deal with the issues of the development of new ideas, products and processes points to the firm's technology orientation. An organisation's strategic stance incorporating a defined technology policy has been often analysed as a determinant of innovation (Wilson *et al.*, 1999). Lindman (2002) also used a measure of technology policy to gauge the innovative efficiency of SMEs in the Finnish metal industry. He suggests strong R&D orientation, active search for new technological knowledge, product uniqueness and products with technological newness and large application scope as indication of high technology orientation. It is also believed that an organisation's active acquisition of new technologies in itself should be considered innovative, as they can then employ them to develop new products (Cooper, 1984, 1994), and integration of innovation and technological considerations with strategic development is beneficial (Soderquist *et al.*, 1997). Spitsberg *et al.* (2013:27) believe that "a systematic process for building technology awareness and articulating and disseminating knowledge within the organization is critical for enabling a collaborative cross-functional ideation process" necessary for open innovation success.

Cooperation and networks

One of the more recent advances in understanding the SME sector has been the role of networks in their functioning. It is widely believed that successful SMEs use cooperative networks to compensate for their individual weaknesses. It thus seems natural that successful innovators amongst SMEs may also be using such networks to accomplish the tasks associated with innovation, which are generally more difficult for them in comparison to the large business. Dickson & Hadjimanolis (1998:5) argued, "Since small firms typically lack some of the essential resources for innovation . . . they have to acquire them from external sources. . . . Thus, the management of inter-organisational relationships and networking in general is critical for successful innovation by small firms". In the same vein, Ren *et al.* (2013:17) stated that "an inter-organizational network is considered to be an alternative for internal innovation because it can both reduce the economic risks associated with innovation and increase the pool of diverse resources needed to introduce new products successfully".

The network perspective provides a more complete account of the innovation activities of small firms, as is shown by Rothwell (1992). This perspective clearly demonstrates that a firm's innovation strategies influence and are in turn influenced by the conduct and strategic stance of other agencies in the network (Bull, 1993).

Barnett & Story (2000) believed that to gain and maintain a global competitive advantage, small firms should possess certain specific assets which most of them usually lack. They, however, can compensate for this by using various modes of collaboration with a wide range of players in the environment. This is how the advantage of collaboration can neutralise the adverse outcomes of throttling competition and diseconomies of scale (Raco, 1999). In this context, it is noted that high-tech firms are more likely to have an explicit and planned strategy of cooperation (Brush & Chaganti, 1996).

Frenz *et al.* (2004) cited the TRACES and HINDSIGHT projects in the US and the SAPPHO project in the UK as examples of the importance of cooperation and networks of advice and information for successful innovation, and recommend that public policy to promote such cooperation is called for. They claim that innovation by firms depends upon and is enhanced by cooperation and collaboration, both between firms and with other bodies, such as universities and networking between firms and their suppliers, customers or even competitors. In high-tech sectors, these types of alliances are very common. These alliances enhance the firm's innovative performance through a complex network of people relationships that boost learning, channel information flows and help coordination by creating trust and by redressing conflict of interest (Moss Kanter, 1994). Referring to Kitson *et al.*'s (2003) work on data from surveys conducted by the ESRC's Centre for Business Research (CBR), Frenz *et al.* (2004) reported that half of the innovating firms but just one-sixth of the noninnovating firms engaged in collaborative partnerships. From the CBR data, it also appears that the overall impact of increased innovation and collaboration leads to enhanced rates of growth of output and employment, both for the individual firm and for the whole economy.

Scotland's good historic performance as a novel product and process innovator despite low intramural investment in R&D is attributed partly to Scottish innovators' higher propensity to enter into cooperative arrangements for innovation with universities and research organisations (Frenz *et al.*, 2004). However, the validity of such explanation is questioned in Chapter 5 in light of evidence from various sources, including the research reported in this book.

Managerial efficiency

Innovation can be seen as one of the managerial functions to be performed, not as frequently for the small firm as manufacturing or marketing but certainly quite often if it wishes to gain and maintain some competitive advantage. For this, the entrepreneur and the key decision makers in the firm must possess a unique and diverse set of managerial skills and capabilities (Beaver & Jennings, 2000 and Jennings & Beaver, 1997).

What makes the demands of innovation more complex is that unlike other managerial functions, innovation is considered a skill difficult to impart. Thus, a business which has, generally, poor managerial calibre is more likely to compromise an innovation project than the one which has high managerial efficiency. Therefore, the search has been on for analysing the skills needed by an SME to be a successful innovator.

Research analysing the inability of small firms to be consistently innovative indicates inadequate marketing and management skills (Moore, 1995). Beaver & Prince (2002), referring to the works of Grieve-Smith & Fleck (1987), explained that small firms have serious problems in obtaining and grooming requisite managerial talent since they cannot afford the pay and prerequisites that the large firms usually provide. The managerial inefficacy thus obviously springs from financial inadequacy suffered by the small firms. They claim that unless small firms have the functional experts or high internal capabilities, information search and consequent managerial action can be extremely expensive, misdirected and myopic. Freel (1998) believed that management competency is one of the two main skill constraints affecting SMEs innovation. Works on factors inhibiting small-firm innovation consistently indicate low levels of general management, particularly, marketing management skills (Moore, 1995). Being a complicated process, innovation presupposes a certain level of management calibre. Managerial inadequacies within SMEs, such as poor planning and financial judgement, thus make innovation impossible (Barber *et al.*, 1989). The other indicated managerial deficiencies include insufficient delegation, high turnover of managerial staff (Nooteboom, 1994) and excessive dependence on word-of-mouth sales without any coordinated marketing effort (Oakey, 1991).

Internal nonstrategic factors

Age

Schumpeter (1934) initiated the work on influence of age of the enterprise on innovation. For this purpose he examined the late 19th-century industrial structure in Europe, where the dominance of small firms was pervasive. He observed that small firms using new technology found it easier to enter an industry. He therefore visualised the small new firms as drivers of innovation and claimed that successful new firms usher in new ideas, products and processes. Their emergence thus disrupts existing arrays of organisation, production and distribution and quasi-rents, resulting from earlier innovations, are eliminated. He refers to this dynamics as 'creative destruction'. This is often referred as *Schumpeter Mark I* pattern of innovation (Fontana *et al.*, 2012).

Size

The work on the relationship between innovation and the size of firm is also pioneered by Schumpeter (1942). In this later work, he takes a position, now popularly referred to as *Schumpeter Mark II* pattern of innovation (Fontana *et al.*, 2012), diametrically opposite of the one he earlier articulated in 1932 and which posits that in relation to small firms, large firms have a higher probability of innovation. Using their financial resources, large firms engage in R&D projects, accumulating in the process technical expertise in their areas of specialisation and thus using innovation as a barrier to entry in the industry (te Velde, 2001). Avermaete *et al.* (2003), referring to the subsequent work by Malerba & Orsenigo (1995), Breschi (1999), Le Bars *et al.*(1998)

and Antonelli & Calderini (1999) on the relationship between innovation and firm size, note that later empirical works have thrown up seemingly contradictory outcomes. Citing Le Bars *et al.* (1998) and Grunert *et al.* (1997) they attribute this to researchers having used varying measures of innovation and sampling methods. In some, data is taken from different industries to draw general conclusions, whereas, in others, the focus is on industry-specific innovation. Moreover, the firms' size distributions differ from sample to sample, and often the very small firms are kept out of analyses.

Human resources

Some analysts have advocated a people-centric approach to the analysis of innovation. They claim that success in innovation is people-dependent rather than resource-dependent (Rothwell, 1983, 1992), and it is the nature and quality of its workforce that determines whether a business is able to innovate or not. Freel (1999:146) has tried to measure skill constraints faced by a small business and its impact on its ability to innovate. He argued that "skills constraints to innovation within small firms are generally thought to be of two principal types: management competency and skilled labour". More recently, KPMG's *Aiming to Grow in 2005* survey reported that 33% of Scottish SMEs believed that skill shortages had a detrimental impact on their new product development efforts (SFDF Manifesto, 2007).

Innovative people

One of the important works recently has been the development of a four-factor confluence model of employee innovation (Patterson, 2001). The model incorporates personality, motivation and intellect aspects of people and uses the factors, (1) Motivation to Change, (2) Challenging Behaviour (3) Consistency of Work Styles and (4) Adaptation. Based on 11 field studies, it demonstrates high predictive validity, where Motivation to Change and Challenging Behaviour are positively related to innovation and Consistency of Work Styles and Adaptation are negatively related to it. Of these, Motivation to Change has emerged as the best person-level indicator of creativity and innovation across a variety of organisations.

Financial resources

One of the perennial problems with which a typical small firm grapples throughout its existence, and particularly so at inception, is inadequacy of resources that spring from financial insufficiency. For a fledgling enterprise, even incremental innovation often needs resources beyond its grasp. The ability of a small firm to innovate thus depends very crucially on its ability to manage resources needed for innovation. As explained earlier, one of the most direct impacts of financial inadequacy is on the ability to of a small firm to recruit the right kind of people, which in turn affects its ability to innovate. The literature shows that SMEs face serious constraints in recruiting, training and retaining a competent and qualified managerial workforce due to the lack of capacity to compete in labour markets, the inability to pay high wages, high costs of staff training and continuous poaching by large firms (Westhead & Storey, 1996 and Oakey, 1997). The fact that these demands are made over and above the costs of routine production and market development prove too prohibitive for SMEs.

Determinants of innovation: External characteristics

External industry-specific factors

The industry-specific factors that have been analysed by scholars relate to the nature of competition in the industry that is influenced particularly by factors such as concentration and barriers to entry (Kraft, 1989 and Dijk *et al.*, 1997).

Schumpeter (1942) argued that high barriers to entry and industrial concentration motivate innovation by restricting competitive initiative and enhancing profitability. This in turn provides the requisite financial resources for R&D and gives an impetus to innovation.

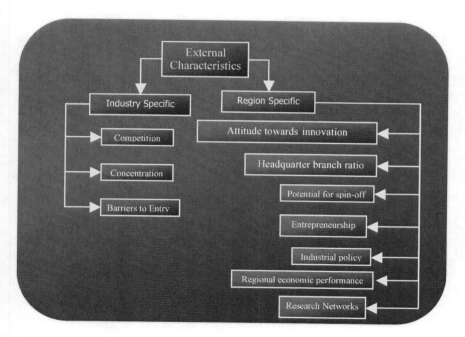

Figure 2.3 External determinants of innovation

On Schumpeter's side of the argument, though not exactly reiterating the ease of innovation caused by a lack of competition but rather highlighting difficulties of innovation under stiff competition, it is asserted that too much competition may dampen tendencies to innovate and seriously restrict a firm's innovative action (Kamien & Schwartz, 1982); it would inhibit rather than promote product innovation (Abernathy & Utterback, 1978) and may encourage firms to try and gain competitive advantage through routes other than product innovation (Fritz, 1989).

On the other side of the divide, it is contended that in the absence of competition, innovation becomes unnecessary (Dasgupta & Stiglitz, 1980) and barriers to entry decrease the incentive to be the product pioneer (Kraft, 1989)

External region-specific factors

SMEs' innovation, very often, has been studied with a regional focus. For instance, in *Belgium* (Avermaete *et al.*, 2003), *Central London*, (Georgellis *et al.*, 2000), *China* (Xie *et al.*, 2010), *Cyprus* (Dickson & Hadjimanolis, 1998), *Finland* (Lindman, 2002), *France* (Soderquist *et al.*, 1997 Lecerf, 2012), *Greece* (Salavou *et al.*, 2004), *Ireland* (Doran *et al.*, 2012), *Italy* (D'Angelo, 2012), *Mexico* (Martinez *et al.*, 2013), *Northern Ireland*, (McAdam *et al.*, 2004), *Poland* (Klonowski, 2012), *Portugal* (Fontes & Coombs, 1996), *Spain* (Carmen *et al.*, 2006)*The Netherlands*, (Engelen, 2002 and van Hemert, 2013), *Turkey* (Burgess *et al.*, 1998), *UK* (Boyle 1998 and Freel, 1999; Woodcock *et al.*, 2000; Stockdale 2002 and Frenz *et al.*, 2004) and *Wisconsin*, US (Blumentritt, 2004).

In one of the early works on the regional dimension of innovation, Oakey (1979) reported that in all planning regions of the UK there was a strong tendency for short distance intraregional movement of innovations, which highlights the importance of developing indigenous regional innovation potential.

In an analysis based on 300 important innovations introduced by the UK firms between 1956 and 1978, Oakey *et al.* (1980) showed that branch plants do not produce their expected share of innovation. They conclude that new techniques are more likely to be developed and manufactured on site if the plant concerned is a headquarter factory while 'branch' plants are more likely to 'import' products developed elsewhere.

In their seminal work on small firm innovation, Rothwell & Zegveld (1982) try to address the issue of whether innovation, and particularly small-firm innovation, is a regional phenomenon. They report the following:

1   A country's propensity for technological innovation is determined not only by the economic conditions prevailing there and its R&D infra-structure but also by the society's attitude towards innovation. Cultural differences between different countries and regions strongly affect the

rate and direction of technical change as well as government policies set up to foster innovation.

2   Independent small firms might be better vehicles for regional development than the branch manufacturing plants of large firms. Large companies tend to establish centralised R&D laboratories, thus localising innovative effort, often at the site of patent establishment, which can make it difficult for branch plants to innovate in response to local market needs.

3   The markets of independent small firms are often localized, thus making small firm innovation largely a local phenomenon; this is well illustrated in the UK.

Later explorations on the regional context of small firm innovation found the following:

1   Apart from economic performance, the political, technological and institutional settings of a region determine the potential of its innovative milieu (Camagni, 1991).

2   New technology-based firms that are located in science parks grow faster than do independent companies (Heydebreck, 1997).

3   "Innovative SMEs do better when they are part of a community or cluster of like-minded firms" Beaver & Prince, (2002:31).

4   Legislation and industrial policy in the region, public research institutes, universities, membership of industry-wide associations and other forms of networking influence a firm's innovative conduct (Antonelli & Calderini, 1999, Breschi, 1999 and Avermaete *et al.*, 2003).

The process perspective to innovation

Another strand of scholarly work on innovation analyses the *process* of innovation. From this point of view, innovation is visualised as a chain of events, not necessarily chronological, that culminates in successful new product or process development.

It is argued that the process perspective to the phenomenon of innovation, particularly amongst SMEs, is more meaningful and relevant than its determinant-based view because of its sensitivity to the 'micro-processes of innovation' and its ability to explain 'the embededness of innovation in SMEs' (Edwards *et al.*, 2005).

The argument that only through a process perspective can one capture the essence of the relationship between management practice at the level of a firm and its external environment is a focus of research which has remained underdeveloped in the existing literature of innovation in SMEs (Edwards *et al.*, 2005). It also helps in a better understanding of "the individual entrepreneur, her or his venture and its context by considering them jointly" (Johannisson & Monsted, 1997:113).

Nooteboom's (2000) observation that managerial learning leads to the development of structures through application of ideas in evolving contexts is consistent with a process perspective, which explains how some routines, innovations and ideas, over a period, gradually emerge as a dominant design or a best practice leading to their application, often with variations in myriad contexts.

The seminal work on product development process by Cooper (1990) and his stage-gate model, shown in Figure 2.4, is the best-known example of this genre. Cooper (1990:44) described a stage-gate system as "both a conceptual and an operation model for moving a new product from idea to launch". The basic thought behind the stage-gate approach is that the new product development process passes through many stages, such as assessment, business case preparation, development, testing, validation and market launch. Before it can enter a particular stage, it must pass through a 'gate', or pass a test of having fulfilled all criteria that are designated to ensure that the project is worthy of going forward. Failing these tests, the project is stopped and improved enough to pass these tests subsequently and go through the 'gate' to reach the next stage, or else it must be killed. The notion behind the stage-gate system is that if a project were tested for its further potential at every stage of development, then ideas without merit would not use up resources only to eventually prove failures. Through such continuous testing of the merit of product development projects, the company would be able to focus on ideas that will eventually succeed, in the process, making the product development process more successful and cost effective.

Cooper's work concerns the large corporation and looks at innovation from a high-tech perspective. As will be explained later in this book, the process of innovation in small low-tech enterprises is similar to the one

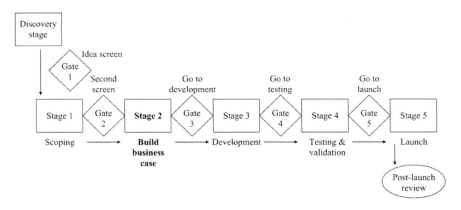

Figure 2.4 An overview of the stage-gate system
Source: Cooper, 2008

described by Cooper in some respects and different in others. Though the process theory literature is not exclusively a stage-based analysis of innovation, stage thinking has dominated this perspective. As the impact on practice is an important virtue of a good theory (Whetten, 1989) and the impact of stage-gate models is undeniable, both in terms of the extent of their widespread use as well as the reported gains from their use (Ettlie & Elsenbach, 2007 and Barczak *et al.*, 2009), their pivotal place within the process theory literature is irrefutable. Among their weaknesses, however, are oversimplification of reality through a linear visualisation of the innovation process and their inability to capture the overlapping and concurrent nature of innovation events (Brockhoff, 1999). Recently, Cooper (2008) has tried to address these critiques and proposed more flexible 'xpress', 'lite' and 'spiral' variations.

Definition, taxonomy and perspectives to innovation: A critique

Definition: The innovation span

The description of innovation in the literature encompasses a wide range of perspectives. A closer examination, however, reveals that the definitional writing on innovation collectively captures several aspects of a large span of innovation-related overlapping actions and outcomes. Through Figure 2.5, a new conceptual construct, the *innovation span*, is presented, within which all notions and definitions of innovation can be accommodated. This concept is based on the premise that all innovation definitions recognise, implicitly or explicitly, that new ideas are at the core of a chain of events that culminate in innovation and deliver its consequent payoffs. It is also generally accepted that during the process of innovation ideas are refined and transformed into useful new products, processes or organisations. The process sometimes steers the business into new markets, or allows it to use new inputs. Despite a plethora of definitions of innovation, there is no real disagreement amongst the scholars on the essential nature and consequences of innovation described previously. The apparent lack of settled opinion on the definition of innovation results from scholars and organisations including in their definitions only certain segments of the full *innovation span*. For instance, as shown in Figure 2.5, Brenner (1990) and Frenz & Oughton (2005) discuss only segments II and III, Schumpeter (1934), European Commission (1995) and Edquist (2001) focus on segments III and IV, OECD (1981) incorporates segments I, II and a part of segment III, Oslo Manual (OECD 1997) considers segments I, II and III whereas West & Farr (1990) include segments III, IV and V.

The idea of *innovation span* not only clarifies the apparent conflict in the meaning of innovation, it can also provide a wider and yet congruent context to all works on innovation by identifying at the outset, the components of the *innovation span*, they are concerned with.

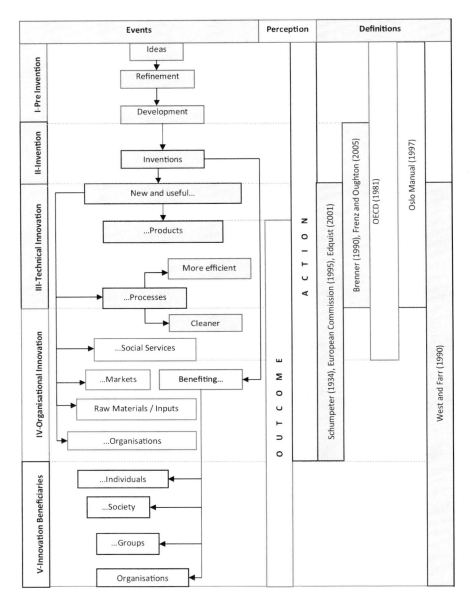

Figure 2.5 The innovation span

The *innovation span* also provides a mechanism to compare the previous research on innovation and brings into sharp relief the futility of comparison of works concerning noncommon segments of the *innovation span*. In addition, it has the flexibility of incorporating any new segments or components emerging from future work, not included here, by linking them to the span at appropriate points.

Taxonomy

Despite a seeming exclusivity of classification reflected in the taxonomy discussed in literature, there is an overlap between some of the different classes of innovation. For instance, it is generally not possible to create an absolutely new product without a concomitant, albeit sometimes marginal change in existing processes. Similarly, a new production process usually alters, again sometimes only marginally, the existing products. As the source of competitive advantage is in the product as well as in the process, in most cases, innovative firms bring about simultaneous change in both, and therefore innovation at the level of a firm has elements of product as well as process components, and the separation between the two suggested by the above taxonomy is not always observed. Similarly, absolutely new products, unrelated, in any way, to the existing ones are created so rarely that almost all innovation, in a way, is incremental.

It should be noted in this context that product and process innovation have been explored more often and in-depth than organisational innovations. The reason is that data on R&D has been easily available to be used as a convenient proxy for product and process innovation. However, as will be explained in Chapter 5, the use of R&D as a proxy for innovation is problematic as R&D investment is generally a poor predictor of innovation performance of businesses. Two reasons are apparently responsible for it. Not all R&D results in successful product or process development, and all product and process innovations do not necessarily need R&D investments. Another significant issue in this context is that innovative performance of businesses depends on both volume and efficiency of R&D effort, and data on R&D expenditure shows only its volume and not its efficiency.

Innovation perspectives: Process versus determinants

Despite the arguments listed earlier on the relative appropriateness of a process-centric perspective over a determinants-based view of innovation in SMEs, it would not be wise to ignore completely the existing work on the determinants of innovation. Analysing SMEs innovation from a combined process cum determinant perspective and linking the results of such effort to the extant literature is a more meaningful approach. In this book, such an approach is used.

Conclusions

It is obvious that definitional endeavour on innovation has generated a large number of perspectives to the phenomenon of innovation. There has not been any attempt to unify these diverse notions of innovation. Such an attempt is made here by conceptualising the idea of an *innovation span*. It would be churlish to claim that it settles the conflict in understanding of innovation but it does represent advancement in our understanding of innovation. As explained above, the notion of *innovation span* allows all work on innovation, including the work contained in this book, to be juxtaposed in a wider and yet congruent context.

Efforts to ascertain the factors affecting the success of innovation in business organisations have produced a large number of influences. Depending on their research focus and the data availability, innovation scholars have tried to conceptualise a number of determinants and verify their impact on innovation performance of businesses in a region, in an industry or in a group of enterprises chosen, based on some other suitable criteria. Major determinants of innovation reported in literature are classified here, starting with the broad categories of internal and external characteristics of enterprise. Internal characteristics are then divided into strategic and nonstrategic variables, whereas the external determinants are classified into region and industry-specific factors.

This effort allowed crystallisation of this research inquiry. As this inquiry is on innovation and new product development in the Scottish food SMEs, the pursuit of external characteristics of business as an innovation influence is automatically ruled out. The search here, therefore, is for the internal characteristics of case study enterprises that played a role in shaping the direction, pace and outcome of their innovative efforts. It also attempts to discover into what part of taxonomy of innovation, discussed in the literature, does the Scottish food SMEs innovations fit.

In the previous research, the phenomenon of innovation is attempted to be understood from one more perspective. The process perspective analyses it as a chain of events culminating in innovation. From the process viewpoint, the moot question that this book tries to answer is that if a number of small Scottish food companies have successfully created new products, then is there an identifiable underlying process through which they all have passed? Following Bygrave (1989), 'the enlightened speculation' here is that there should be one common process, with minor variations. The reasoning is that these companies are similar on many counts. Each of them is small, Scottish, in the food sector and a successful product innovator. It therefore seems intuitively appealing that they would have similar strengths, drawbacks and scope in their efforts to create new goods. The process that they use to develop new products therefore must have many common threads. Therefore, here an attempt is also made to uncover these common threads as well as explain any chain of causality of that might be linking them with one another.

References

Abernathy, W and Utterback, J (1978) Patterns of industrial innovation, *Technology Review*, 80(7):41–7

Angle, H L (1989) Psychology and organisational innovation, in Van De Ven, A H, Angle, H L and Pool, M S (Eds) *Research on the Management of Innovation*, New York: Harper & Row, 135–70

Antonelli, C and Calderini, M (1999) The dynamics of localised technology change, in Gambardella, A and Malerba, F (Eds) *The Organisation of Economic Innovation in Europe*, New York: Cambridge University Press, 158–76

Avermaete, Tessa, Viaene, Jacques, Morgan, Eleanor J and Crawford, Nick (2003) Determinants of innovation in small food firms, *European Journal of Innovation Management*, 6(1):8–17

Barber, J, Metcalfe, J and Porteous, M (1989) Barriers to growth: The ACARD study, in Barber, J, Metcalfe, J and Porteous, M (Eds) *Barriers to Growth in Small Firms*, London: Routledge

Barczak, G , Griffin, A and Kahn, K (2009), Trends and Drivers of Success in NPD Practices: Results of the 2003 PDMA Best Practices Study, *Journal of Product Innovation Management*, 26(1):3–23

Barnett, Elizabeth and Storey, John (2000) Managers' accounts of innovation processes in small and medium-sized enterprises, *Journal of Small Business and Enterprise Development*, 7(4):315–25

Beaver, G and Jennings, L (2000) Small business, entrepreneurship and enterprise development, *Journal of Strategic Change*, 9(7):397–405

Beaver, Graham and Prince, Christopher (2002) Innovation, entrepreneurship and competitive advantage in the entrepreneurial venture, *Journal of Small Business and Enterprise Development*, 9(1):28–37

Blumentritt, Tim (2004) Does small and mature have to mean dull? Defying ho-hum at SMEs, *Journal of Business Strategy*, 25(1):27–33

Boyle, Emily (1998) Entrepreneurship and the changing structure of estate agency in the UK, *Journal of Small Business and Enterprise Development*, 5(2):141–50

Brenner, Reuven (1990) *Rivalry: In Business, Science, Among Nations*, New York: Cambridge University Press

Breschi, S (1999) Spatial patterns of innovation: Evidence from patent data, in Gambardella, A and Malerba, F (Eds) *The Organisation of Economic Innovation in Europe*, New York: Cambridge University Press, 71–103

Brockhoff, Klaus (1999) *Produktpolitik*, Fourth Edition, Stuttgart: UTB

Brush, C G and Chaganti, R (1996) Co-operative strategies in non-high-tech new ventures: An exploratory study, *Entrepreneurship, Theory and Practice*, 21(2):37–55

Bull, A (1993) *Entrepreneurial Textile Communities*, London: Chapman & Hall

Burgess, T F, Gules, H K, Gupta, J N D and Tekin, M (1998) Competitive priorities, process innovations and time-based competition in the manufacturing sectors of industrialising economies: The case of Turkey, *Benchmarking for Quality Management & Technology*, 5(4):304–16

Bygrave, W (1989) The Entrepreneurship paradigm (I) A philosophical look at its research methodologies, *Entrepreneurship Theory and Practice* 14(1):7–26

Camagni R (1991) Local milieu, uncertainty and innovation networks: Towards a new dynamic theory of economic space, in Camagni, R (Ed) *Innovation Networks Spatial Perspectives*, London: Belhaven Press

Carmen, C, María de la Luz, F and Salustiano, M (2006) Influence of top management team vision and work team characteristics on innovation: The Spanish case, *European Journal of Innovation Management*, 9(2):179–201

Cavanagh, R E and Clifford, D K (1983) Lessons from America's mid-sized growth companies, *The Mckinsey Quarterly*, (Autumn):2–23

Cohen, W M and Levinthal D A (1990) Absorptive capacity: A new perspective on learning and innovation, *Administrative Science Quarterly* 35(1):128–52

Cooper, Robert G (2008) Perspective: The Stage-Gates Idea-to-Launch Process – Update What's new, and NexGen systems, *Journal of Product Innovation Management*, 25(3): 213–32

Cooper, R G (1984) New product strategies: What distinguishes the top performers?, *Journal of Product Innovation Management*, 1(2):151–64

Cooper, R G (1990) Stage-gate systems: A new tool for managing new products, *Business Horizons*, 33(3):44–54

Cooper, R G (1994) New products: The factors that drive success, *International Marketing Review*, 11(1):60–76

Cooper, R G and Kleinschmidt, E J (1993) Stage gate system for new product success, *Marketing Management*, 1(4):20–29

Cooper, R G and Kleinschmidt, E J (2000) New product performance: What distinguishes the star products, *Australian Journal of Management*, 25(1):17–45

Daft, R L (1978) A dual-core model of organisational innovation, *Academy of Management Journal*, 21(2):193–210

Damanpour, F (1987) The adoption of technological, administrative and ancillary innovation impact of organisational factors, *Journal of Management*, 13(4): 675–88

Damanpour, F and Evan, W M (1984) Organisational innovation and performance: The problem of organisational lag, *Administrative Science Quarterly*, 29(3):392–409

D'Angelo, Alfredo (2012) Innovation and export performance: A study of Italian high-tech SMEs, *Journal of Management and Governance*, 16(3):393–423

Dasgupta P and Stiglitz, J (1980) Industrial structure and the nature of innovative activity, *Economic Journal*, 90(358):266–93

Dewar, R D and Dutton, J E (1986) The adoption of radical and incremental innovations an empirical analysis, *Management Science*, 32(11):1422–33

Dickson, K E and Hadjimanolis, A (1998) Innovation and networking amongst small manufacturing firms in Cyprus, *International Journal of Entrepreneurial Behaviour & Research*, 4(1):5–17

Dijk, B V, Hertog, R D, Menkveld, B and Thurik, R (1997) Some new evidence on the determinants of large- and small-firm innovation, *Small Business Economics*, 9(4):335–43

Dodgson, M and Rothwell, R (1991) Technology strategies in small firms, *Journal of General Management*, 17(1):45–55

Doran, Justin, Jordan, Declan and O'Leary, Eoin (2012) The effects of the frequency of spatially proximate and distant interaction on innovation by Irish SMEs, *Entrepreneurship and Regional Development*, 24(7/8):705–27

Dosi, Giovanni (1988) Sources, procedures and microeconomic effects of innovation, *Journal of Economic Literature*, 26(3):1120–71

Dougherty, Deborah and Heller, Trudy (1994) The illegitimacy of successful product innovation in established firms, *Organisation Science*, 5(2):200–18

Edquist, Charles (2001) *The systems of innovation approach and innovation policy: An account of the state of the art,* Lead paper at the DRUID Conference, Aalborg, June 12–15

Edwards, Tim, Delbridge, Rick and Munday, Max (2005) Understanding innovation in small and medium-sized enterprises: A process manifest, *Technovation,* 25(10):1119–27

Engelen, Ewald (2002) How innovative are Dutch immigrant entrepreneurs? Constructing a framework of assessment, *International Journal of Entrepreneurial Behaviour & Research,* 8(1/2):69–92

Ettlie, J E and Elsenbach J A M (2007). Modified stage-gate regimes in new product development, *Journal of Product Innovation Management,* 24(1):20–33

Ettlie, J E and Bridges, W P (1982) Environmental uncertainty and organisational technology, *IEEE Transactions on Engineering Management,* 29(1):2–10

Ettlie, J E, Bridges, W P and O'Keefe, R D (1984) Organisational strategy and structural differences for radical versus incremental innovation, *Management Science,* 30(6):682–695

European Commission (1995) *The Green Paper on Innovation,* Luxembourg, Sweden: Commission of the European Communities

European Commission (2004) *Innovation in Europe: Results for the EU, Iceland and Norway Data 1998–2001,* Luxembourg, Sweden: Commission of the European Communities

Fontana, Roberto, Nuvolari, Alessandro, Shimizu, Hiroshi and Vezzulli, Andrea (2012) Schumpeterian patterns of innovation and the sources of breakthrough inventions: Evidence from a data-set of R&D awards, *Journal of Evolutionary Economics,* 22(4):785–810

Fontes, Margarida & Coombs, Rod (1996) New technology-based firm formation in a less advanced country: A learning process, *International Journal of Entrepreneurial Behaviour & Research,* 2(2):82–101

Freel, M (1998) Evolution, innovation and learning: Evidence from case studies, *Entrepreneurship and Regional Development,* 10(2):137–49

Freel, Mark S (1999) Where are the skills gaps in innovative small firms? *International Journal of Entrepreneurial Behaviour & Research,* 5(3):144–54

Freeman, C (1974) *The Economics of Industrial Innovation,* Harmondsworth, UK: Penguin Books

Frenz, Marion and Oughton, Christine (2005) *Innovation in the UK regions and devolved administrations: A review of the literature,* Final Report for the Department of Trade and Industry and the Office of the Deputy Prime Minister

Frenz, Marion, Michie, Jonathan and Oughton, Christine (2003) Regional dimension of innovation: Results from the Third Community Innovation Survey, *International Workshop Empirical Studies on Innovation in Europe,* Faculty of Economics, Urbino, Italy: University of Urbino

Frenz, Marion, Michie, Jonathan and Oughton, Christine (2004) *Cooperation and innovation: Evidence from the community innovation survey,* Unpublished paper

Fritz, W (1989) Determinants of product innovation activities, *European Journal of Marketing,* 23(10):32–43

Georgellis, Yannis, Joyce, Paul and Woods, Adrian (2000) Entrepreneurial action, innovation and business performance: The small independent business, *Journal of Small Business and Enterprise Development,* 7(1):7–17

Godin, B (2003). *The Rise of Innovation Surveys: Measuring a Fuzzy Concept, Project on the History and Sociology of STI Statistics, International Conference in Honour of K. Pavitt "What We Know About Innovation"*, University of Sussex, Brighton, UK: SPRU

Grieve-Smith, A and Fleck, V (1987) business strategies in small high technology companies, *Long Range Planning*, 20(2):61–8

Grunert, K G, Brunso, K and Soren, B (1997) Food-related lifestyle: Development of a cross-culturally valid instrument for market surveillance, in Kahle, L and Chiagouris, C (Eds) *Values, Lifestyles, and Psychographics,* Mahwah, NJ: Erlbaum, 337–54

Hall, B (2005) Innovation and diffusion, in Fagerberg, J, Mowery, D C and Nelson, R (Eds) *The Oxford Handbook of Innovation,* Oxford, UK: Oxford University Press, 459–85

Heydebreck, Peter (1997) *Technological Interweavement: A means for new technology-based firms to achieve innovation success,* in Jones-Evans, Dylan and Klofsten, Magnus (Eds) *Technology, Innovation and Enterprise: The European Experience,* London: Macmillan Press

Hollander, S (1965) *The Sources of Increased Efficiency: A Study of DuPont Rayon Plants,* Cambridge, MA: MIT Press

Hopkins, Jim (2001) When Designers Ignore Consumers, Products Can Flop, *USA Today,* December 31

Hurley, R F and Hult, G T M (1998) Innovation, Market Orientation and Organisational Learning: An Integration and Empirical Examination, *Journal of Marketing,* 62(3): 42–54

Jennings, L and Beaver, G (1997) The performance and competitive advantage of small firms: A management perspective, *International Small Business Journal,* 15(2):63–75

Johannisson, B and Monsted, M (1997) Contextualising entrepreneurial networking, *International Studies of Management and Organisation,* 27(3):109–37

Kamien, M I and Schwartz, N L (1982) *Market Structure and Innovation,* Cambridge: Cambridge University Press

Kimberly, John R and Evanisko, Michael J (1981) Organisational innovation: The influence of individual, organisational and contextual factors on hospital adoption of technological and administrative innovations, *The Academy of Management Journal,* 24(4):689–713

Kitson, M, Michie, J and Sheehan, M (2003) Markets, competition, cooperation and innovation, in Coffey, D and Thornley, C (Eds) *Industrial and Labour Market Policy and Performance,* London: Routledge

Klonowski, Darek (2012) Innovation propensity of the SME sector in emerging markets: Evidence from Poland, *Post-Communist Economies,* 24(1):133–43

Knight, K E (1967) A descriptive model of the intra-firm innovation process, *Journal of Business,* 40(4):478–496

Kraft, K (1989) Market structure, firm characteristics and innovative activity, *Journal of Industrial Economics,* 37(3):329–36

Le Bars, A, Mangematin, V and Nesta, L (1998) *Innovation in SMEs: The missing link,* Paper Presented at the High Technology Small Firms Conference, University of Twente, Enschede

Lecerf, Marjorie-Annick (2012) Internationalization and innovation: The effects of a strategy mix on the economic performance of French SMEs *International Business Research,* 5(6):2–13

Lewrick, Michael, Omar Maktoba and Williams, Robert L Jr (2011) Market orientation and innovators' success: An exploration of the influence of customer and competitor orientation, *Journal of Technology Management & Innovation*, 6(3):48–61

Lindman, Martti Tapio (2002) Open or closed strategy in developing new products? A case study of industrial NPD in SMEs, *European Journal of Innovation Management*, 5(4):224–36

Malerba, F and Orsenigo, L (1995) Schumpeterian patterns of innovation, *Cambridge Journal of Economics*, 19(1):47–65

Mansfield, E (1968) *The Economics of Technological Change*, New York, NY: W W Norton

Mansfield, E (1971) *Research and Innovation in the Modern Corporation*, New York, NY: W W Norton

Martinez, Serna, Maria, del Carmen, Maldonado Guzman, Gonzalo and Pinzon Castro, Sandra Yesenia (2013) The relationship between market orientation and innovation in Mexican manufacturing SMEs, *Advances in Management and Applied Economics*, 3(5):125–37

McAdam, Rodney, Mcconvery, Thomas and Armstrong, Gren (2004) Barriers to innovation within small firms in a peripheral location, *International Journal of Entrepreneurial Behaviour & Research*, 10(3):206–21

Mckee, D (1992) An organisational learning approach to product innovation, *Journal of Product Innovation Management* 9(3):232–45

Mezias, S J and Glynn, M A (1993) The three faces of corporate renewal: Institution, revolution and evolution, *Strategic Management Journal*, 14(2):77–101

Montoya-Weiss, M M and Calantone, R (1994) Determinants of new product performance: A review and meta-analysis, *Journal of Product and Innovation Management*, 11(5):397–417

Moore, B (1995) What differentiates innovative small firms?, *Innovation initiative paper No. 4*, ESRC Centre for Business Research, Cambridge, UK: University of Cambridge

Morgan, R E, Katsikeas, C S and Appiah-Adu, K (1998) Market orientation and organisational learning capabilities, *Journal of Marketing Management*, 4(4):353–81

Moss Kanter, R (1994) Collaborative advantage, *Harvard Business Review*, 72(4):96–108

Nonaka, I and Takeuchi, H (1995) *The Knowledge Creating Company*, Oxford: Oxford University Press

Nooteboom, B (1994) Innovation and diffusion in small firms: Theory and evidence, *Small Business Economics*, 6(5):327–47

Nooteboom, B (2000) *Learning and Innovation in Organisations and Economies*, Oxford: Oxford University Press

O'Gorman, Colm (1997) Success strategies in high growth small and medium-sized enterprises, in Jones-Evans, Dylan and Klofsten, Magnus (Eds) *Technology, Innovation and Enterprise: The European Experience*, Basingstoke: Macmillan

Oakey, R (1991) Innovation and the management of marketing in high technology small firms, *Journal of Marketing Management*, 7(4):343–56

Oakey, R (1997) *A review of policy and practise relating to high technology small firms in the UK*, Manchester Business School Working Paper, No. 359

Oakey, R and S Cooper (1991) The relationship between product technology and innovation performance in high technology small firms, *Technovation*, 11(2):79–91

Oakey, R P (1979) *An analysis of the spatial distribution of significant British industrial innovation,* Discussion Paper No. 25, Centre for Urban and Regional Development Studies, University of New Castle Upon Tyne

Oakey, R P., Thwaites, A T and Nash, A. (1980) the regional distribution of innovative manufacturing establishments in Britain, *The Journal of the Regional Studies Association,* 14(3):235–53

OECD (1981) *The Measurement of Scientific and Technical Activities: Proposed Standard Practice for Surveys of Research and Experimental Development,* Paris: OECD, 15

OECD (1997) *The Oslo Manual: Proposed Guidelines for Collecting and Interpreting Technology Innovation Data,* Paris: OECD

Patterson, F (2001) *The Innovation Potential Indicator: Test Manual and User's Guide,* Oxford, UK: Oxford Psychologists Press

Pavitt, K (1991) Key characteristics of the large innovative firm, *British Journal of Management,* 2(1):41–50

Raco, M (1999) Competition, collaboration and the new industrial districts: Examining the institutional turn in local economic development, *Urban Studies,* 36(5/6):951–69

Ren, Shenggang, Wang, Longwei, Yang, Wei and Wei, Feng (2013) The effect of external network competence and intrafirm networks on a firm's innovation performance: The moderating influence of relational governance, *Innovation: Management, Policy & Practice,* 15(1):17–34

Roberts, E (1991) Strategic transformation and the success of high-technology companies, *International Journal of Technology Management, Special publication on the Role of Technology in Corporate Policy,* 59–80

Rothwell, R (1983) Innovation and Firm Size: A case for dynamic complementarily– or is small really beautiful? *Journal of General Management,* 8(3):5–25

Rothwell, R (1992). Successful industrial innovation: Critical success factors for the 1990s, *R&D Management,* 22(3):221–39

1Rothwell, Roy and Zegveld, Walter (1982) *Innovation and the Small and Medium Sized Firm: Their Role in Employment and in Economic Change,* London: Frances Pinter

Rubera, Gaia and Kirca, Ahmet H (2012) Firm innovativeness and its performance outcomes: A meta-analytic review and theoretical integration, *Journal of Marketing,* 76(3):130–47

Salavou, H, Baltas, G and Lioukas, S (2004) Organisational innovation in SMEs: The importance of strategic orientation and competitive structure, *European Journal of Marketing,* 38(9/10):1091–1112

Schumpeter, Joseph A (1934) *The Theory of Economic Development,* Cambridge: Harvard University Press

Schumpeter, Joseph A (1942) *Capitalism, Socialism and Democracy,* New York: Harper & Row

SFDF Manifesto (2007) Scottish Food and Drinks Federation, www.sfdForGuk/sfdf/SFDF_manifesto_12pp_v8.pdf, accessed on 25 September 2007

Smith, Adam (1776) *The Wealth of Nations,* Edited by Edwin Cannan, 1904 Reprint Edition 1937, New York: Modern Library

Soderquist, Klas, Chanaron, J J and Motwani, Jaideep (1997) Managing innovation in French small and medium sized enterprises: An empirical study, *Benchmarking for Quality Management & Technology,* 4(4):259–272

Spitsberg, Irene, Brahmandam, Sudhir, Verti, Michael J and Coulston, George W (2013) Technology landscape mapping: At the heart of open innovation, *Research-Technology Management*, 56(4):27–35

Stata, R (1989). Organisational learning–the key to management innovation, *Sloan Management Review*, 30(3):63–74

Stockdale, B (2002) *Regional Breakdown of the UK Innovation Survey 2001*, www.dti.gov.uk/files/file9672.pdf, accessed on 23 July 2007

te Velde, R. A. (2001) *Schumpeter's theory of economic development revised*, Paper Presented at the ECIS Congress on the Future of Innovation Studies, Eindhoven

Temin, P (1979) Technology, regulation and market structure in the modern pharmaceutical industry, *Bell Journal of Economics*, 10(2):426–46

Utterback, J M (1971) The process of technological innovation within the firm, *Academy of Management Journal*, 14(1):75–88

Van de Ven, A M, Angle, H L and Poole, M S (Eds) (1989) *Research on the Management of Innovation: The Minnesota Studies*, New York: Harper & Row

van Hemert, Patricia, Nijkamp, Peter and Masurel, Enno (2013) From innovation to commercialization through networks and agglomerations: Analysis of sources of innovation, innovation capabilities and performance of Dutch SMEs, *Annals of Regional Science*, 50(2):425–52

Vyas, Vijay (2005) Imitation, Incremental Innovation and Climb Down: A strategy for survival and growth of new ventures, *Journal of Entrepreneurship*, 14(2):103–16

West, M A and Farr, J L (Eds) (1990) *Innovation and Creativity at Work*, Chichester: Wiley

Westhead, P and Storey, D (1996) Management training and small firm performance: Why is the link so weak? *International Small Business Journal*, 14(4):13–24

Wheelwright, Steven C and Clark, Kim B (1992) Competing through development capability in a manufacturing-based organisation, *Business Horizons*, 35(4):39–43

Whetten, D A (1989) What constitutes a theoretical contribution? *Academy of Management Review* 14(4): 490-95

Wilson, A L, Ramamurthy, K and Nystrom, C (1999) A multi-attribute measure for innovation adoption: The context of imaging technology, *IEEE Transactions on Engineering Management*, 46(3):311–21.

Woodcock, D J, Mosey, S P and Wood, T B W (2000) New product development in British SMEs, *European Journal of Innovation Management*, 3(4):212–21

Xie, X M, Zeng, S X and Tam, C M (2010) Overcoming barriers to innovation in SMEs in China: A perspective based cooperation network, *Innovation: Management Policy and Practice*, 12(3):298–310

Zirger, Billie J and Maidique, Modesto A (1990) A model of new product development: An empirical test, *Management Science*, 36(7):867–83

3 Methodology

This investigation of new product development in the Scottish food SMEs generates and tests a set of propositions and suggests a number of policy prescriptions. It also distils a discernible pattern of innovation from the observations of the investigated companies and discusses the possibilities of implementing them in presently noninnovative small food companies. The investigation thus extends past intellectual curiosity and aims not merely to build a theory of a less understood phenomenon but also to explore its potential in improving the practice. As explained in Chapter 2, this inclination played a role in shaping the research agenda for this investigation and thereby influenced its methodological remit.

The method

The main body of this book and its principal conclusions are derived by using qualitative case study research, and they spring from an exploratory rather than a confirmatory quest (Onwuegbuzie & Teddlie, 2003). The conclusion so derived are subsequently triangulated through a wider survey of Scottish companies of varying size that have successfully developed new products, in food as well as nonfood sectors.

Robert Yin (213:13) in his seminal treatise, described case study research as "... an empirical enquiry that investigates a contemporary phenomenon within its real life context, especially when the boundaries between phenomenon and context are not clearly evident". Case studies usually depict an authentic, though summarised record of events, the main players concerned and other influencing variables, and generally have 'an institutional focus' (Roselle, 1996). As a research strategy, the focus of case studies is unravelling the nature of dynamics present within situations. They are especially valuable when the laboratory type of controls are not feasible and/or ethically unjustified (Miles & Huberman, 1994 and Remenyi *et al.*, 1998). Affording a flexible and often an opportunistic research approach is the obvious strength of case studies. It can, however, also turn out to be its chief drawback, especially if the research process is not very well documented. However, if this could be managed, as is the attempt here, then the flexibility allowed by the case study research fits well with the classical research cycle of 'description, explanation and testing' (Meredith, 1993) and can generate useful insights.

Though the principal use of case study research is to collect data, its main utility is in building theories (Eisenhardt, 1989 and Eisenhardt & Graebner, 2007). Case studies, being the chronicles of real activities at a point in space and time, are of immense value in theory construction, particularly in exploratory research, such as the one documented here. The notion that even properly executed case studies are not rigorous enough is not true. They are, in fact, quite difficult to carry out, and the impression that they are a 'soft' research option is misleading (Yin, 1994 and Patton & Appelbaum, 2003).

Case studies are often based on a limited number of cases. If, however, a serious intellectual effort is made to understand the nature and consequences of interaction between various components of the systems and the components themselves, it is possible to generalise from few or even a single case reasonably well (Normann, 1984), a result, I hope, that is achieved here. Case study research often discovers intricate details of subjects under study, shows up crucial relationships between core components and is particularly valuable in the absence of any strong theory to depend on (Bozeman & Klein, 1999), as is the case here. More importantly, case study research is better equipped than survey methods to answer the 'whys' and 'hows', as it can probe more acutely the conduct and motivation of people than can structured surveys (Westgren & Zering, 1998) and satisfies all the core tenets of quality research, and inhabits a vital niche in management science (Patton & Appelbaum, 2003).

Though the case study research has the distinct merit as discussed previously, particularly for exploratory studies, it has been often criticised on grounds that it generates 'soft' data, is unable to establish causality conclusively and is based on limited observations (Swartz & Boaden, 1997). It is thus often alluded that case study research lacks rigour, may be biased, is prone to *ad hoc* theory generation (Seuring, 2008) and is incapable of conventional 'scientific generalisation' (Remenyi *et al.*, 1998). However, it is important to note in this context that case study research aims at creations of generalisation for theoretical propositions (analytical generalisation), which is the purpose here, and not generalisations for populations or universes (statistical generalization) (Yin, 1994).

Though some of these critiques spring from, I would argue, an unreasonable expectation from the case study research to deliver what it does not promise, some of it is a reflection on poorly executed case study research, which, unfortunately, forms a significant part of research in this genre. To guard against the present study falling prey to such a fate, following precautions were taken:

1   Multiple case studies are conducted to avoid lack of rigour and *ad hoc* theorisation.
2   Broad theoretical propositions and not an all-inclusive theory are aimed at, and

3   a theoretical – and not a random – sample (Eisenhardt, 1989) of com-
     panies is chosen that have significant common characteristics.

The knowledge gap

As shown earlier, research, over the last 50 years has consistently linked
innovation with business success. Much of this work, however, concerns
large corporations and/or analyses innovation from a high-tech perspective. Innovative endeavours of people in traditional low-tech SMEs have
not received similar attention, and academics have generally ignored these
'lacklustre' enterprises (Menrad, 2004 and Sankaran & Mouly, 2007). My
search for post-2000 studies on innovation in food SMEs revealed only
six journal articles (Avermaete *et al.*, 2003; Ngamkroeckjoti *et al.*, 2005;
Bhaskaran, 2006; Russo Spena & Colurcio, 2010; Muscio *et al.*, 2010 and
Colurcio *et al.*, 2012). When we consider that innovation activities influence
growth in low-tech small firms as well (Petrou & Daskalopoulou, 2009),
and the firms in low-tech and medium-tech industries contribute more to
economic growth than do high-tech sectors even in the developed countries
(Von Tunzelmann & Acha, 2005 and Hirsch-Kreinsen, 2008), along with
the preponderance of SMEs in the global food industry, the need for exploratory investigations of innovation in small companies in this sector becomes
obvious.

The epistemological foundation of inquiry

Like all human conduct, academic research is based, overtly or otherwise, on
some philosophical outlook. Neglecting a philosophical perspective, though
not necessarily lethal, can acutely affect the value of consequent research
(Amaratunga & Baldry, 2001).

The four paradigms of research methodology on which much of academic research is grounded are positivism, realism, critical theory and
constructivism.

The *positivist* approach, reflecting, principally, a quantitative orientation,
is based on the belief that a unit of investigation should always be mea-
sured objectively. The two chief characteristics of the positivist's approach
are independence of the researcher from the subject and the formulation of
a hypothesis for testing. Positivism is grounded in the premises of causal
relationship and elemental laws, and usually trims down the investigated
entity into smaller and simpler components to facilitate analysis (Easterby-
Smith *et al.*, 2001)

The *realistic* approach, sometimes referred to as 'phenomenological'
or 'inductive' research, assumes the reality to be 'holistic and socially con-
structed', which cannot be determined objectively. Realist researchers attempt
to comprehend and elucidate a phenomenon. They do not seek to discover

any external causes or elemental laws (Remenyi *et al.*, 1998). Most qualitative techniques are grounded in a realistic methodological paradigm.

Critical theory presumes that all political, economic, social or cultural reality is comprehensible. It visualises investigators and their subjects to be interactively interlinked and assumes that the system of belief of investigators influences their inquiry through a discourse between the researchers and their subjects. It thus is based on the notion that all knowledge is subjective and value-dependent, and all research outcomes are influenced by the personal values of the researchers (Riege, 2003).

The *constructivist* approach to research is based on the assumption of manifold comprehensible realities, grounded empirically as well as socially in an ethereal intellectual outlook of individuals (Riege, 2003). It aims at enhancing the understanding of the uniqueness as well as the diversity of constructions that researchers and their subjects originally hold (Anderson, 1986). The chief constructivist belief is that all knowledge is 'theory-driven', independence of researchers from their research subjects or objects is not possible and theory and practice are interdependent (Mir & Watson, 2000).

As very little work has been previously done on the theme explored in this book, an exploratory research approach based on a realist-inductive paradigm was therefore chosen. This concedes to Bygrave's (1989:18) premise that "at the beginnings of a paradigm, inspired induction (or more likely enlightened speculations) applied to exploratory, empirical research may be more useful than deductive reasoning from them", and Churchill & Lewis' (1986) position that in the absence of theory generation from close empirical examination, the 'hypo-deductive approaches' prevent the development of requisite understanding of processes, activities and outcomes.

Case study design

To underpin the case studies, a conceptual framework reflecting the 'prior theory' (Perry, 1998), distilled from a review of extant literature, was first built. In the next phase, a set of open-ended questions whose answers would inform the conceptual framework were identified. This effort, translated the theoretical framework couched in academic idiom into a set of questions that laypeople can understand and respond to.

It is often claimed that there are no exact norms on the optimum number of cases in multiple case studies (Perry, 1998), and it is not easy to know if the number of cases analysed are enough for generalisation (Swartz & Boaden, 1997). Eisenhardt (1989), however, advised analysing between 4 and 10 cases. She argued that it is generally quite arduous to build a theory of adequate complexity from less than four cases. On the other hand, more than 10 cases generates so much data that analysing them becomes extremely difficult. It was thus tentatively decided to carry out case studies of between five to nine Scottish food companies for this research.

The research process

Unlike positivist-confirmatory research, where conclusions can be rigorously tested using statistical methods that have greater acceptability within the social science research circles, case study research remains in constant need to establish the validity of its processes and outcomes. One way to achieve this is to "make explicit the process involved in collection and analysis of data" (Shaw, 1999: 59). All steps of the research process adopted to arrive at the results of this research are thus described here in detail. The description is in the form of a 'true chronology' and not as 'reconstructed logic' (Silverman, 1985). The objective is to underpin the inductive, or 'Verstehen', (Outhwaite, 1975) nature of analysis used here.

As was discussed previously, the initial phase of the inquiry was based on a set of open-ended questions arising from the conceptual model, which itself emerged from a review of extant literature. However, occasionally it became necessary to return to the extant literature as issues sprang up from the fieldwork, which necessitated a reexamination of previous research to modify the conceptual model to accommodate the observed reality. This, to a limited extent, altered the nature of discussion with subsequent respondents. This also meant that the early respondents were required to be contacted again.

For identification of innovative small food companies in Scotland, input from Mrs Susan Laing and Mr Aidan Craig, from the Entrepreneurship Centre of Edinburgh Napier University, who both have long and distinguished records of work with Scottish SMEs, as well as from contacts within the food and drinks cluster in Scottish Enterprise, the business support agency of the Government of Scotland, proved useful. From these sources, names of small food companies that had successfully created new food products in the recent past were obtained. From these, 12 organisations that had more frequently come out with new products were short-listed. The rationale for applying this norm was that companies that introduced new products more regularly should have enduring structures to sustain the process of innovation, whereas those that developed new products only occasionally may have an element of chance in their innovation process, which will then be difficult to capture and articulate. This brought within our purview some truly innovative organisations, and the fact became increasingly clear as their investigation commenced and continued.

To start the process, letters were sent to the managing directors of each short-listed company, explaining the nature of this inquiry and requesting permission to interview the people who had a good understanding of the process of new product development in their enterprises. Nine out of 12 identified companies agreed to let us interview the people directly involved in new product development, the 'key informants' to the inquiry. Targeting these key informants sharpened the focus of the investigation by 'not randomly sampling from the universe of characteristics under study' but by 'selectively sampling specialised knowledge' (Tremblay, 1982).

It is not known why some companies did not agree to participate in this research. However, it can be surmised that they were perhaps not convinced that they could gain anything from the exercise. It may also be so that there are elements in their new product development process that they did not want to divulge. As the investigated case study companies were willing to discuss every aspect of innovation in their organisations quite openly, it is difficult to understand a reason for that, if at all, this was the case.

Out of nine companies that agreed to participate in the research, in one case only a telephone interview was possible and the information that could be recorded was not sufficiently detailed to be included here. In another case, it turned out that the company employed more than 250 people. Though the key informants in this company were interviewed in the first phase, the resultant information did not go in the final analysis. This book thus is based on findings from seven case study companies.

In most cases, interviewees were the owners/entrepreneurs themselves, and some were senior executives, but in every case these were people directly involved with new product development in their organisations in leadership roles.

The case study companies

The case study companies for this research comprised seven enterprises, all located within Scotland. They are identified only as Company A, Company B and so on in order not to compromise the confidentiality of information they provided.

As Figure 3.1 and Figure 3.2 show, the group of companies chosen for case studies more or less replicates this highly diversified product profile of the Scottish food industry. This establishes two facts, each quite significant. One, this indeed is a representative sample of the diversity of the Scottish food industry, and two, innovation amongst the Scottish food companies occurs in all food categories.

Table 3.1 The case study companies

Companies	Age	Main products	Employment
A	35	Pizzas	50
B	25	Pâté	70
C	23	Bakery, confectionery	130
D	13	Ice cream	14
E	32	Haggis, soups, candies, jam	03*
F	17	Seafood, smoked salmon	190
G	9	Organic soups and ready meals	40

*Outsources most of its activities

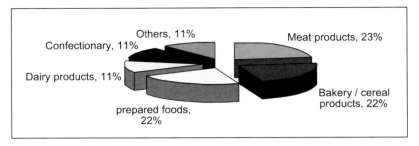

Figure 3.1 The case study companies

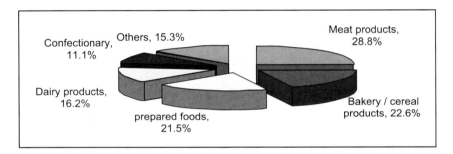

Figure 3.2 Scottish food market, 2004
Source: Leatherhead Food International, 2005

Data collection

Some of the basic information on the case study companies was gathered from sources in the public domain, such as company websites and the UK government's business information service 'Companies house'. However, much of substantive information came through interviewing the key informants. A questionnaire to test for innovativeness of key people involved with new product development in investigated organisations was also served and analysed.

Two teams of interviewers conducted four interviews each, and on each team there were at least two interviewers. This followed Eisenhardt's (1989) advice on the use of multiple data collection teams, à la Pettigrew (1990), allowing for a more objective perspective to the evidence when the data was cross-shared within the research team. All respondents were contacted on many subsequent occasions to fill information gaps or to provide further information.

All except the first interviews were carried out at the manufacturing sites of identified food companies, and all but two were recorded on a digital tape recorder so as to listen to conversations many times over in order to 'penetrate (the) internal logic' and 'interpret the subjective understanding of reality' (Shaw, 1999), as narrated by the 'key informants'. Prior to interviewing, a brief outline of the research project and its overall objectives was provided to all respondents, and they were assured that any information that they supplied would not be divulged without their permission. On each occasion, apart from conducting the semi-structured interviews, a tour of the site was undertaken. Recorded interviews were later transcribed verbatim. Depending on the needs of research, the style of transcription of interviews falls somewhere between two terminal types: "Naturalism, in which every utterance is transcribed in as much detail as possible and denaturalism, in which idiosyncratic elements of speech (e.g., stutters, pauses, nonverbals, involuntary vocalizations) are removed" (Oliver *et al.*, 2005:1273–74). As the interest was in the 'informational content' (MacLean *et al.*, 2004) of conversation, a denaturalistic transcription style was followed and 'idiosyncratic elements' were ignored. In case of two nonrecoded interviews, detailed notes were taken during the interviews.

In transcribed and summarised form, the collective evidence provided a unique insight, not merely into the process of innovation in these companies but also a look into the world of some exceptionally creative individuals and the functioning of their organisations. Though the broad themes of this research came from the literature review and the consequent 'enlightened speculation' (Bygrave, 1989), many other themes emerged during the process of interviewing. The final set of themes became evident during the process of reading and rereading this document. This is an experience previously reported by other qualitative researchers, such as Bradley *et al.* (2007:1761), who explain that "reviewing data without coding helps identify emergent themes without losing the connection between concepts and their context".

Data analysis

"The analysis of case study evidence is one of the least developed and most difficult aspects of doing case studies" (Yin, 2009:127). There are no set rules of inductively analysing qualitative data, and so it is important to explain how the raw data was converted into findings. This is explained below.

As all respondents answered the same set of open-ended questions that formed the semi-structured interviews, *within case analysis* has not been difficult. The only issue has been reporting the evidence in case of two interviews that were hand recorded where the opportunity to quote the respondents verbatim has been absent. The process during within-case analysis has essentially been of distilling the discussion to filter out information unrelated to any form of substantive inquiry and colleting all relevant information under various themes of inquiry.

For cross-case analysis, several blank Microsoft Word files, titled by each theme that emerged from *within-case analysis,* were created and kept simultaneously open on a PC desktop. Each interview transcription and each interview summary was then carefully read one at a time, and anything mentioned that related to any specific theme of inquiry were copied and pasted in the file on the theme. When the process was complete, each file contained all the raw cross-case comparison data that the investigation had generated on each theme. All evidence collated on each theme was then considered together to see the nature of evidence and if all evidence pointed to a single pattern, or if there were more than one patterns. In case of differing patterns, the presence of any explanatory influence was then searched for. After the process was complete, each file was converted into a coherent text explaining the themes. The text was also interspersed with the quotes from transcriptions as well as phrases from interview summaries for subsequent readers to verify that the assertions made were consistent with the evidence from the interviews to 'explicate how we claim to know what we know' (Altheide & Johnson, 1994).

Triangulation survey

The verification of the model of product innovation derived from the case studies was subsequently undertaken through a triangulation survey of Scottish companies that have successfully developed new products. The details of the survey process, methods used and survey results are provided in Chapter 7 of this book.

References

Altheide, D L and Johnson, J M (1994) Criteria for assessing interpretive validity in qualitative research, in Denzin, N K and Lincoln, Y S (Eds) *Handbook of Qualitative Research*, London: Sage, 485–99

Amaratunga, D and Baldry, B (2001) Case study methodology as a means of theory building: Performance measurement in facilities management organisations, *Work Study*, 50(3):95–104

Anderson, F (1986) On method in consumer research: A critical relativist perspective, *Journal of Consumer Research*, 13(2):155–77

Avermaete, Tessa, Viaene, Jacques, Morgan, Eleanor J and Crawford, Nick (2003) Determinants of innovation in small food firms, *European Journal of Innovation Management*, 6(1):8–17

Bhaskaran, Suku (2006) Incremental innovation and business performance: Small and medium-size food enterprises in a concentrated industry environment, *Journal of Small Business Management*, 44(1):64–80

Bozeman, B and Klein, Hake (1999) The case study as research heuristic: Lessons from the R&D value mapping project, *Evaluation and Programming Planning*, 22:91–103

Bygrave, W (1989) The entrepreneurship paradigm (I) A philosophical look at its research methodologies, *Entrepreneurship Theory and Practice*, 14(1):7–26

Churchill, N C and Lewis, V L (1986) Entrepreneurship research directions and methods, in Sexton, D L and Smilor, R L (Eds) *The Art and Science of Entrepreneurship*, Cambridge, MA: Ballinger, 333–65

Colurcio, Maria, Wolf, Patricia, Kocher, Pierre-Yves and Russo Spena, Tiziana Russo (2012) Asymmetric relationships in networked food innovation processes, *British Food Journal,* 114(5):702–27

Easterby-Smith, M, Thorpe, R and Lowe, A (2001) *Management Research: An Introduction,* Second Edition, London: Sage

Eisenhardt, K M (1989) Building theories from case study research, *Academy of Management Review,* 14(4):532–550

Eisenhardt, Kathleen M and Graebner, Mellissa A (2007) Theory building from cases: Opportunities and challenges, *Academy of Management Journal,* 50(1):25–32

Hirsch-Kreinsen, Hartmut (2008) "Low-Tech" innovations, *Industry and Innovation* 15(1): 19–43

MacLean, Lynne, Mechthild, Meyer and Alma, Estable (2004) Improving accuracy of transcripts in qualitative research, *Qualitative Health Research,* 14(1):113–23

Menrad, K (2004) Innovations in the food industry in Germany, *Research Policy,* 33(6/7): 845–78

Meredith, J (1993) Theory building through conceptual methods, *International Journal of Operations and Production Management,* 13(5):3–11

Miles, M B and Huberman, A M (1994) *Qualitative Data Analysis: An Expanded Sourcebook,* Second Edition, London: Sage

Mir, R and Watson, A (2000) Strategic management and the philosophy of science: The case for a constructivist methodology, *Strategic Management Journal,* 21(9):941–53

Muscio, Alessandro, Nardone, Gianluca and Dottore, Antonio (2010) Understanding demand for innovation in the food industry, *Measuring Business Excellence,* 14(4):35–48

Ngamkroeckjoti, Chittipa, Speece, Mark and Dimmitt, Nicholas J (2005) Environmental scanning in Thai food SMEs: The impact of technology strategy and technology turbulence, *British Food Journal,* 107(5):285–305

Normann, R (1984) *Service Management,* New York: Wiley

Oliver, Daniel G, Serovich, Julianne M and Mason, Tina L (2005) Constraints and opportunities with interview transcription towards reflection in qualitative research, *Social Forces,* 84(2):1273–89

Onwuegbuzie, A J & Teddlie, C (2003) A framework for analyzing data in mixed methods research. In Tashakkori A & Teddlie C (Eds.) Handbook of mixed methods in social and behavioral research, Sage, Thousand Oaks, CA: 351–83

Outhwaite, W (1975) *Understanding Social Life: The Method Called Verstehen,* London: George Allen and Unwin

Patton, Eric and Appelbaum, Steven H (2003) The case for case studies in management research, *Management Research News,* 26(5):61–71

Perry, C (1998) Processes of a case study methodology for post graduate research in marketing, *European Journal of Marketing,* 32(9/10):785–802

Petrou, Anastasia and Daskalopoulou, Irene (2009) Innovation and small firms' growth prospects: Relational proximity and knowledge dynamics in a low-tech industry, *European Planning Studies,* 17(11):1591–1604

Pettigrew, Andrew M (1990) Longitudinal field research on change: Theory and practice, *Organization Science,* 1(3):267–92

Remenyi, D, Williams, B, Money, A and Swartz, E (1998) *Doing Research in Business and Management: An Introduction to Process and Method,* London: Sage

Riege, Andreas M (2003) Validity and reliability tests in case study research: A literature review with hands-on applications for each research phase, *Qualitative Market Research: An International Journal,* 6(2):75–86

Roselle, A. (1996) The case study method: A learning tool for practising librarians and information specialists, *Library Review,* 45(4):30–38

Russo Spena, Tiziana and Colurcio, Maria (2010) A cognitive-relational view of innovation in the agri-food industry: The fresh-cut business, *International Journal of Innovation Management,* 14(2):307–29

Sankaran, Jayaram K and Mouly, Suchitra V (2007) Managing innovation in an emerging sector: The case of marine-based nutraceuticals, *R&D Management,* 37(4):329–44

Seuring, Stefan A (2008) Assessing the rigor of case study research in supply chain management, *Supply Chain Management: An International Journal,* 13(2):128–37

Shaw, Eleanor (1999) A Guide to the Qualitative Research Process: evidence from a small firm study, *Qualitative Market Research: An International Journal,* 2(2):59–70

Silverman, D (1985) *Qualitative Methodology in Sociology,* Aldershot, UK: Gower

Swartz, E and Boaden, R (1997) A methodology for researching the process of information management in small firms, *International Journal of Entrepreneurial Behavior & Research,* 3(1):53–65

Tremblay, M (1982) The key informant technique: A non-ethnographic application, in Burgess, R G (Ed) *Field Research: A Sourcebook and Field Manual,* London: George Allen and Unwin, 97–104

von Tunzelmann, N and Acha, N (2005) Innovation in low tech industries, in Fagerberg, J, Mowery, D C and Nelson, R R (Eds) *The Oxford Handbook in Innovation,* Oxford: Oxford University Press

Westgren, R and Zering, K (1998) *Case study research methods for firm and market research,* Proceedings of Research Conference of Food and Agricultural Marketing Consortium, Park City, UT:

Yin, R (1994) *Case study research: Design and methods,* Second Edition: Sage Publishing,

Yin, R K (2003) *Case study Research: Design and Methods,* Third Edition, Thousand Oaks, CA: Sage Yin, R K (2009) *Case Study Research: Design and Methods,* Fourth Edition, Thousand Oaks, CA: Sage

4   Context of study I

The Scottish food and drinks industry: An overview

Introduction

The Scottish food and drinks industry comprises several distinctive segments. These include *beverages,* which are principally alcoholic drinks but also in significant proportions soft drinks, coffee, tea, fruit juices and bottled water; *meat and seafood,* which includes both raw and processed varieties, sold in fresh as well as frozen conditions; *milk and milk derivatives,* including butter, cream, yoghurt, desserts and ice cream; *bakery products,* like bread, rolls, biscuits and cakes; *breakfast cereals, savoury snacks, confectionary* and *prepared foods,* such as ready-to-eat meals, soups, sauces, spreads and pizzas (Leatherhead Food International, 2005). The alcoholic beverages segment, as shown in Figure 4.1, however, dominates the industry.

As is obvious from the previous description, the food and drinks industry in Scotland manufactures and markets practically every variety of food item consumed in the UK and other developed countries. Apart from being a producer and exporter of some iconic products like Scotch whisky and Scottish salmon, it also produces and exports many characteristically Scottish dishes, such as haggis.

Employment

The food and drinks sector is one of the biggest employers of people in Scotland. In 2010, it employed 3% of the total and 25% of all the manufacturing workforce in Scotland (Scottish Government, 2012a). If we consider employment in the entire food and drink supply chain, then employment in this sector rises to about 23% of total employment in Scotland (Scottish Government, 2012b). Employment in the food and drinks area, however, along with that in the rest of manufacturing, has been falling for quite some time in Scotland, and the trend is forecast to continue. As the decline is likely to be significantly less in food and drinks than in other manufacturing sectors, the ratio of employment in this sector to total Scottish manufacturing employment should increase further in years to come.

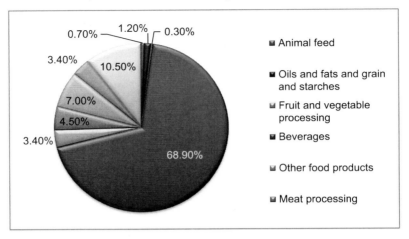

Figure 4.1 Scottish food and drinks industry segments
Source: Food and drinks in Scotland: Key Facts, 2012

Businesses

In 2010, the manufacture of food products and beverages in Scotland comprised about 1,100 businesses dominated by SMEs, and 81% of these employed less than 50 workers. Most of these are family businesses that supply quality niche products and use locally sourced ingredients. Scotland also has a thriving agricultural sector, with a substantial share in national agricultural output. It produces 80% of the UK's fish catch, holds 30% of its beef herd and supplies 10% of its liquid milk.

Exports

In 2011, the industry had a turnover of £13 billion, of which about £5.3 billion, nearly 40%, was exported, making it the most export-intensive industry in the country (Scotland Food & Drink, no date, a). In 2012, exports from the food and drinks industry constituted 39% of all Scottish manufacturing exports in the year (Scottish Government, 2014). The Scottish food and drinks exports go to a wide range of destinations in nearly 200 countries. The US is its biggest export market, followed by France and Spain. Regionally, 70% of Scottish exports go to other EU countries. Since 1996, however, exports to Eastern Europe has been rising, making it go up from the sixth to the second most popular region for exports of Scottish food and drinks. Export of its renowned shellfish, smoked salmon, game and other foods is worth over £500 million annually. The major part of its exports, over 70% of total, however, is alcoholic beverages, principally whisky, whereas fish accounts for 59% of all food exports (Scottish Government 2012b). Food and drinks manufacturing exports from Scotland have been growing consistently for quite some time, including during the period of recent recession. In 2012, food and drinks was the number one exporting industry in Scotland, growing at a compound rate of 5% between 2002 and 2012; exports from the sector were the fastest growing manufacturing exports from Scotland (see Figure 4.2; Scottish Government 2014).

Retailing

Total turnover of food and drinks retailers in Scotland was worth £13.1 billion in 2011 (Scotland Food & Drinks, no date, b). The retailing of food in Scotland is principally through grocery superstores, convenience stores and corner shops. Grocery superstores in Scotland had a turnover of over £10 billion in 2012 (Scottish Government, 2012b). The massive sales potential of grocery superstores in Scotland and the UK represents a significant opportunity for innovative small food companies, as will be subsequently explained in this book. According to the Living Costs and Food Survey of the Office for National Statistics, in 2012 food and drinks household expenditure in Scotland constituted 14% of total expenditure, of which 11% was on food and nonalcoholic drinks and a further 3% on alcoholic drinks, tobacco and narcotics.

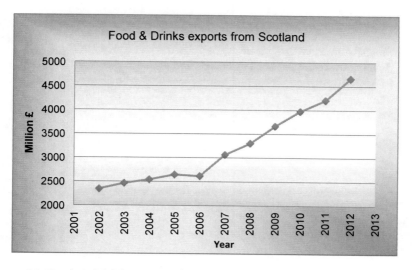

Figure 4.2 Food and drinks exports from Scotland

Source: Graphic generated from Global Connections Survey, various years

Recent trends

A shake-up in the Scottish food and drinks industry has been going on for over a decade. In the post-1998 period, there has been a steady decline in the number of businesses and employment in this sector. In the 12-year period

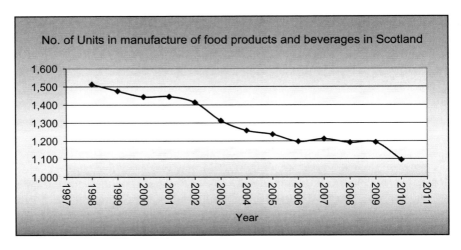

Figure 4.3 Number of units, food and beverages, Scotland
Source: Graphic generated from Scottish Business Statistics, various years

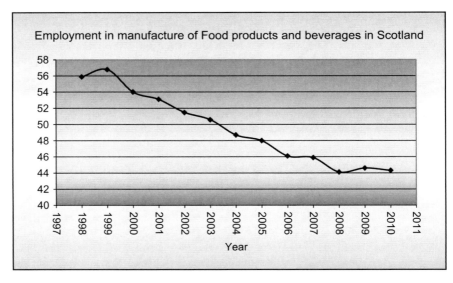

Figure 4.4 Employment, food and beverages, Scotland
Source: Graphic generated from Scottish Business Statistics, 2011

between 1998 and 2010, the number of business units in this sector has declined by 28%, and employment in the same period has declined by 21%.

This trend, however, is not a mark of weakening of this sector. On the contrary, it reflects its rising strength and productivity. It appears that the

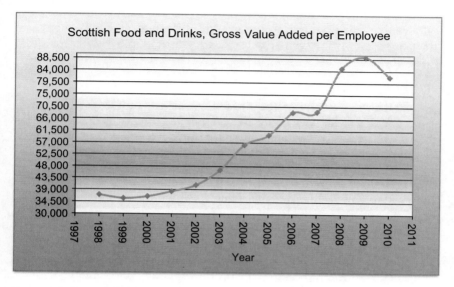

Figure 4.5 Scottish food and drinks, gross value added per employee in GB £
Source: Graphic generated from Scottish Business Statistics, 2011

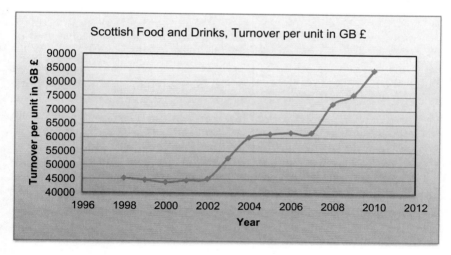

Figure 4.6 Scottish food and drinks, turnover per unit in GB £
Source: Graphic generated from Scottish Business Statistics, 2011

businesses that have closed down and caused a loss of employment in this sector lacked competitive vigour; in the wake of their exit both total turnover and turnover per unit as well as gross value added per employee has increased. Against a 28% and 21% fall in the number of businesses and employment, respectively, during 1998–2010, business turnover in food and beverages manufacturing has grown by 35%, and turnover per unit by a good 121%. The best indicator, however, of the improving productivity of the sector is an 86% rise in gross value added per employee.

Conclusions

Food and drinks is one of the most diversified manufacturing sectors in Scotland and produces virtually every variety of food consumed in the UK. It is also one of the biggest employers of people in Scotland, its most export-intensive sector, its top exporter and the fastest growing export sector.

In this industry, principally made up of SMEs, a shake-up in the post-1998 period has been observed whereby both the number of businesses and employment has declined. This decline is caused by a combination of factors. The relentless growth of supermarkets in Britain has shut down the food companies whose products were in direct competition with the supermarkets. In addition, some companies were not able to cope with increasing regulation of the food industry and related stringent standardisation norms, such as Hazard Analysis and Critical Control Points (HACCP)[1]. These two factors collectively imposed huge demands on the Scottish food companies, and the relatively weaker amongst them closed down. Those that survived this onslaught, however, were able to grow into the space vacated by the closing companies. As a result, during 1998–2010, the turnover per unit grew at a rate of 5% per annum and gross value added per employee by 7% per annum. Competitiveness and adaptability thus seems to have paid off for the surviving manufacturers in this industry. As there are no signs of let-up in the competitive pressures unleashed by the growth of supermarkets, and as the role of innovation in raising competitiveness is now well appreciated, the food and drinks companies in Scotland will have to pay greater attention to innovation if they wish to continue to survive and grow. Study of innovation in this sector now is thus more critical than ever before.

As will be explained later in this book, the growing hold of supermarkets on the grocery trade in the UK is both a challenge and an opportunity for small food companies, and the enterprises investigated in this research have used innovation as an instrument to seize this opportunity to their advantage.

Note

1 Food companies suffered a similar fate in the wake of introduction of HACCP in other countries too; see for instance Khatri & Collins (2007) for an analysis of impact of HACCP on the Australian meat industry.

References

Khatri, Y and Collins, R (2007) Impact and status of HACCP in the Australian meat industry, *British Food Journal,* 109(5):343–54

Leatherhead Food International (2005) The Scottish Food and Drinks Report, Market Intelligence section, Leatherhead Food International, Leatherhead

Scotland Food & Drinks, (no date, a) Our progress in numbers, www.scotland.gov.uk/Resource/0041/00416949.pdf, last accessed on 12/08/2014

Scotland Food & Drinks, (no date, b) Our collective success in numbers, www.scotlandfoodanddrink.org/media/42652/2013-sfd-progress-in-numbers-book-for-web.pdf, last accessed on 12/08/2014

Scottish Government (2012a)Scottish Business Statistics, Edinburgh: Scottish Government

Scottish Government (2012b) Food & Drinks in Scotland Key facts, Edinburgh: Scottish Government

Scottish Government (2014) Scotland's Global Connections Survey, Edinburgh: Scottish Government

5 Context of study II

Business innovation in Scotland

Introduction

There are two ways to assess innovation performance of businesses in a region. One, through an indirect approach, where innovation inputs such as R&D expenditure are used to gauge the level of innovative effort, and two, through a direct approach where innovation outputs, such as number or proportion of enterprises that develop new products, are used. For a long time, the indirect approach was the only accessible route to this end, as data on innovation output was not available. From 1992 onwards, however, innovation output data emerged for the EU from the Community Innovation Surveys that have since been carried out seven times. These new statistics not only sharpen the focus on the level and content of innovation in European nations and regions, they also bring to light, as the following analysis shows, the fact that innovation inputs have not been telling us the true story. Government in Scotland, however, has continued to look at innovation performance of its enterprises through the tinted glass of indirect methods. Consequently, the Scottish Government's vision of innovation remains clouded.

Innovation vision of the Scottish Government

Historically, the policy pronouncements of the Government of Scotland have not made a clear distinction between R&D and innovation. For instance, the *Framework for Economic Development in Scotland* (Scottish Government, 2004) identifies 'R&D and innovation' as *one* (and not two) of its key priorities. Its consultation paper on *Science and Innovation Strategy for Scotland* (Scottish Government, 2006) projects the volume of R&D expenditure as being synonymous with the level of innovation.

More recently, amongst 45 national indicators set for monitoring performance of the Scottish economy, the Scottish Government website[1] lists bridging the gap in R&D with the EU as its number one performance indicator, stating that higher business enterprise R&D is needed for economic growth. One of its consultation documents also claims that "the critical weakness of the Scottish innovation system remains the low number of enterprises involved in formal R&D." (Reid, 2012:v).

It appears that the economic growth model of Scottish Government is based on the premise *R&D-causes-innovation-causes-competiveness-causes-economic growth.*

R&D in Scotland

Three measures of R&D are prevalent in the UK: business enterprise R&D (BERD), government R&D (GovRD) and R&D by institutes of higher education (HERD). A fourth measure, gross expenditure on R&D (GERD), which is the sum of the first three, is used to reflect the general state of R&D in a country or a region. In 2011, GERD in Scotland constituted 1.56% of GDP of Scotland, whereas in the UK as a whole it was 1.94% of GDP. The Scottish BERD constituted 0.56% of the Scottish GDP whereas its UK value was 1.14% of GDP. BERD/GDP ratio for OECD was even higher, at 1.58%, as shown in Figure 5.1.

As stated earlier, documents published by the Scottish Government reflect its concern over low R&D expenditure in Scotland. They also reiterate its belief that high R&D expenditure is required to achieve its goal of a 'more successful Scotland'; one of its recent publications states that "a key driver of innovation is research and development (R&D)" (Scottish Government, 2013:8)

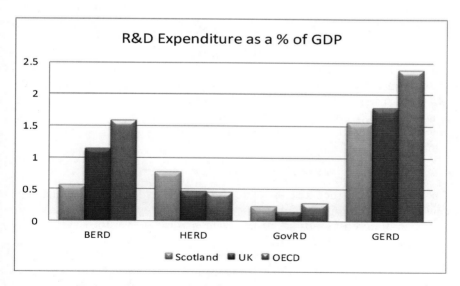

Figure 5.1 R&D as a percentage of GDP, 2011

Scotland's low BERD/GDP ratio, which is less than half of that for the UK, is augmented by its relatively high GovRD and HERD. It may be that the Scottish Government has been maintaining a high (relative to UK) government R&D to prop up low R&D by Scottish businesses to make Scotland more innovative. Though such intention is certainly commendable, the potential efficacy of this strategy is questionable, as there is no evidence of a causal relationship between the volume of R&D expenditure in Scotland and the innovation performance of its businesses. For instance, though BERD as a percentage of GDP in Scotland is less than half of its UK value, as will be shown subsequently in this chapter, innovation performance of Scotland is nearly as good as the UK average. Even more importantly, Scotland, despite having historically a relatively low BERD and low overall R&D, has done exceptionally well as a novel product innovator during the Community Innovation Surveys, CIS_3 (European Commission, 2004) and CIS_4 (Scottish Government, 2007), and as a novel product innovator during CIS_3 than any other UK region.

R&D and innovation in the UK regions

Table 5.1 shows expenditure on two measures of R&D, gross expenditure on R&D (GERD) and business enterprise expenditure on R&D (BERD) in millions of pounds at current prices from 2006 to 2010 in 12 UK regions, and Table 5.2 depicts values of seven indicators of innovation in UK regions in terms of percentage of innovation-active enterprises.

If innovation is indeed R&D-dependent, we should find businesses in regions spending proportionally more on R&D in various forms, exhibiting correspondingly higher innovation. This, however, is not the case, and as shown by the correlation matrix in Table 5.3, correlation between various measures of R&D and innovation is less than benchmark 0.5 in all but two cases. What is most important, however, is that only two sets of correlation from the possible 70 parings are statistically significant either at the 1% or at the 5% level. It can thus be said quite categorically that regional innovation performance of businesses in the UK does not depend on the corresponding extent of regional R&D investment.

Innovation performance of businesses: Scotland versus UK

As mentioned earlier, the only credible direct evidence on regional and national innovation performance of enterprises in output terms comes from the Community Innovation Surveys. The analysis of the 2009 Community Innovation Survey, CIS_6 (Scottish Enterprise, 2012), shows that during the survey period, 54.8% of Scottish firms are innovation-active, whereas in the whole UK this ratio is 58.2%. In comparison, during the 2005 Community Innovation Survey, CIS_4, these ratios were 56.3% for Scotland and 57.1% for the whole of UK. This means that innovation performance of

Table 5.1 R&D in UK regions, millions of pounds at current prices, 2006–2010

	GERD 2006	GERD 2007	GERD 2008	GERD 2009	GERD 2010	BERD 2006	BERD 2007	BERD 2008	BERD 2009	BERD 2010
North East	501	554	551	550	536	292	331	318	308	297
North West	2240	2672	2782	2607	2730	1623	2021	2130	1907	2047
York. & Hu.	900	981	991	1039	1053	384	436	433	452	491
E. Midlands	1358	1458	1381	1454	1589	985	1062	976	998	1143
W. Midlands	1252	1340	1223	1210	1251	915	995	886	847	892
Eastern	4537	4945	5166	4938	4987	3650	3992	4182	3930	3986
London	2659	2914	3049	2962	2957	882	1067	1109	909	902
South East	4803	5153	5185	5509	5574	3347	3515	3466	3698	3758
South West	1901	1836	2017	2022	2113	1232	1229	1345	1277	1362
Wales	493	606	525	530	527	216	308	243	243	244
Scotland	1520	1742	1784	1914	1890	460	543	554	630	622
N. Ireland	317	336	337	478	502	157	177	171	297	324

Source: Scottish Business Statistics, 2012

Table 5.2 Innovation in UK regions, percentage of enterprises, 2008–2010

	Innovation active	Broader innovator	Wider innovator	Product innovator	Process innovator	Product + Process innovator	Product OR process innovator
North East	40.0	41.6	34.9	21.2	12.9	11.7	22.5
North West	32.2	33.6	26.2	18.2	9.5	7.6	20.1
Yorkshire and Hu.	35.6	37.4	28.5	18.0	10.3	7.2	21.1
East Midlands	38.9	40.9	33.0	21.4	10.8	8.2	24.1
West Midlands	38.0	40.7	31.0	18.6	10.8	7.3	22.2
Eastern	41.2	42.7	34.5	20.8	12.7	8.3	25.1
London	32.8	34.2	27.6	17.0	8.8	6.6	19.2
South East	41.2	42.5	34.4	21.8	11.9	8.8	24.9
South West	38.3	40.6	32.8	19.4	9.5	7.4	21.4
Wales	40.6	43.3	32.6	20.1	11.5	8.5	23.2
Scotland	33.3	35.0	29.5	15.2	8.1	5.2	18.1
Northern Ireland	31.8	33.4	26.1	13.0	6.9	4.5	15.4

Source: UK Innovation Survey, 2011

Table 5.3 Correlation matrix: R&D and innovation

		Innovation active	Broader innovator	Wider innovator	Product innovator	Process innovator	Both product AND process innovator	Either product OR process innovator
GERD2006	Correlation	.310	.232	.318	.395	.329	.123	.482
	Sig. (2-tailed)	.327	.469	.314	.204	.297	.704	.112
GERD2007	Correlation	.283	.203	.288	.382	.324	.119	.470
	Sig. (2-tailed)	.373	.526	.364	.220	.304	.713	.123
GERD2008	Correlation	.264	.184	.275	.366	.307	.109	.450
	Sig. (2-tailed)	.407	.568	.387	.242	.332	.737	.142
GERD2009	Correlation	.273	.191	.287	.361	.294	.097	.445
	Sig. (2-tailed)	.391	.552	.366	.249	.354	.764	.147
GERD2010	Correlation	.274	.192	.286	.369	.293	.099	.451
	Sig. (2-tailed)	.390	.549	.368	.238	.355	.761	.141
BERD2006	Correlation	.446	.373	.423	.496	.458	.225	.594*
	Sig. (2-tailed)	.147	.233	.171	.101	.135	.482	.042
BERD2007	Correlation	.409	.335	.381	.480	.447	.219	.577*
	Sig. (2-tailed)	.187	.287	.221	.114	.145	.495	.050
BERD2008	Correlation	.385	.310	.363	.460	.429	.206	.553
	Sig. (2-tailed)	.217	.326	.247	.133	.164	.520	.062
BERD2009	Correlation	.409	.333	.388	.462	.427	.200	.557
	Sig. (2-tailed)	.187	.290	.213	.131	.167	.532	.060
BERD2010	Correlation	.404	.329	.381	.468	.422	.199	.561
	Sig. (2-tailed)	.310	.232	.318	.395	.329	.123	.482

*Pearson correlation significant at the .05 level (two-tailed)

Scottish businesses vis-à-vis the innovation performance of businesses for the whole of UK has deteriorated between 2005 and 2009. This is an obvious cause for concern for the Government of Scotland. Driven by its belief that R&D expenditure is a precursor to improved innovation performance of its businesses, it has thus set raising R&D expenditure in Scotland as its key objective. The fact, however, is that between 2006 and 2009, though gross expenditure on R&D in UK has gone up by 12%, in Scotland it has gone up by 26% and business enterprise R&D, which has gone up by 10% in UK, has gone up by 37% in Scotland, and so there is no doubt that Scotland has been able to achieve its goal of raising business enterprise R&D as well as gross expenditure on R&D. However, the innovation performance of businesses in Scotland, as a result, has not improved but deteriorated vis-à-vis UK. The conclusion is therefore inescapable that the Scottish Government's target of making Scotland a more innovative region by spending more on R&D and by encouraging its businesses to spend more on R&D has not worked. The reason for this failure is obvious. As shown earlier, R&D expenditure is a poor predictor of innovation performance of enterprises, and Scotland cannot hope to become a more innovative region by spending more on R&D.

Another important aspect of innovation in Scotland against its occurrence in the UK is that the relatively marginal underperformance of the Scottish business in relation to the UK average is confined to its smaller firms. Large Scottish enterprises outperform their UK counterparts in most aspects of innovative activities, as is shown in Table 5.4. As business enterprise R&D is undertaken proportionately more by the larger firms, this raises further doubts on the plausibility of the relationship between R&D and innovation.

R&D and innovation in Scotland

Nearly 60% of business R&D in Scotland occurs in pharmaceuticals, consumer electronics, communication equipment, precision instruments, computing and R&D services (Scottish Government, 2012a). In both

Table 5.4 Main innovation indicators by firm size band, Scotland relative to UK = 100, 2009

	10 to 49 employees	50–249 employees	250+ employees
Innovation = active	94	93	110
Product innovator	89	91	91
Process innovator	99	92	121
Wider innovation	96	95	117
Broader innovation	93	100	110

Source: (Scottish Enterprise, 2012)

output and employment terms, these sectors constitute a very small fraction of the Scottish economy. In 2012, the number of enterprises, employment and turnover in the manufacture of basic pharmaceutical products, pharmaceutical preparations, computers, electronics and optical products was around 0.2%, 0.8% and 1.2%, respectively, of all Scottish enterprises (Scottish Government, 2012b). It is difficult to understand how business enterprise R&D, 60% of which is concentrated in about 1% of the Scottish economy, can influence innovation in the rest of its 99%. The fact that 55% of all Scottish enterprises were innovation-active in 2009 makes it obvious that a significant proportion of Scottish businesses innovation is not R&D-driven.

Commercialisation of research by higher education institutes

There is no doubt that Scottish HERD as a percentage of GDP is amongst the highest of all OECD countries, and has been so for many years. However, the contribution of commercialisation and the transfer of knowledge by Scottish universities to the competitiveness of the Scottish economy is negligible. As shown earlier, there is no relationship between money spent in a UK region on R&D and innovation by its businesses. Much of the university research, moreover, is basic, and its evolution into commercially successful products or technologies is a long, complex and uncertain process. A minuscule proportion of all university research is commercialised. Often, researchers would carry away with them their research output, and the fact that Scotland has one of the highest rates of PhD graduates working outside the UK[2] provides no solace. Most importantly, *Higher Education – Business Community Interaction Survey for Scotland* shows that in 2011–2012 there were only 181 active spin-off companies set up by the Scottish HEIs. These enterprises employed 1,998 people and had an annual turnover of over £25 million (HEFCE, 2013). Based on these, as Table 5.5 shows, it is obvious that in the economy of Scotland, university spin-off's economic contribution is practically zero.

Table 5.5 University spin-off's economic contribution, Scotland, 2011–2012

	No. of Units	Employment	Turnover, £
Scotland, total	159,580	1,804,590	243,935,000,000
Active HEIs spinoffs	181	1,998	255,697,000
HEIs spin-offs as a percentage of total	0.11%	0.11%	0.10%

Source: Based on data in *Higher Education – Business Community Interaction Survey, 2011–2012* and Scottish Business Statistics, 2012

Small business innovation in Scotland

The final report of DTZ Pieda consulting on *Scottish Business Attitudes to Research, Development and Innovation* (Scottish Government, 2005:90) describes cases of small innovative companies in Scotland. It reports that there are two types of small innovative companies in Scotland:

> The university spin out and the single site manufacturer or technical consultancy. The University spinouts interviewed appeared to be more of a source of innovative ideas than the single site manufacturer. The single site companies interviewed tended to be undertaking lower level adaptation of existing technology mainly for particular customers to distinguish themselves from the competition and to assist in reducing their costs so that both their products and their service provision can be seen to be competitive. This type of innovation tends to be relatively low risk compared to research being undertaken where an end customer has not been identified.

This report thus identifies two kinds of innovative small companies in Scotland: the university spin-offs, and the low-tech single-site manufacturers, involved in 'lower level adaptation of existing technology'. The *Annual Survey of Small Businesses for Scotland in 2012*[3] reveals that 68% of all small businesses in Scotland introduced new or significantly improved products or services circa 2011. As shown in Table 5.5, university spin-offs in Scotland constitute about 0.11% of its firms. As the Scottish university spin outs employed, on an average, only nine persons in 2012, it can be safely presumed that they are predominantly small firms. As small firms constitute 99% of all Scottish firms, we can say that 67.89% of small Scottish companies that innovated in 2012 therefore must fall in the second category. This is corroborated by the research presented here, where all the investigated small food innovative companies fit the description of the second type. This means that 99.95% of innovation-active small firms in Scotland carry out low-tech innovation without any conventional R&D, and the Scottish Government's perception of R&D-driven high-tech innovation in Scotland is a myth.

The previous research

It is interesting to note in this context that as early as in 1970s, innovation research has shown that R&D is a misleading indicator of innovation, particularly in small firms. Many reasons are cited for this. One, R&D is only one (that, too, a minor) part of the innovation costs and outcomes (Stead, 1976); two, small enterprises usually have no formal R&D departments (Kleinknecht, 1987, Santarelli & Sterlacchini, 1990 and Kleinknecht & Reijnen, 1991) and three, in small firms, R&D has a 'developmental, rather than a fundamental, focus' and is 'spread across a number of functional units, rather than captured (largely) within a single R&D function' (Sterlac-chini, 1999). Despite this and more recently despite acceptance by Scottish Enterprise, the enterprise support agency of Government of Scotland that

> ". . . while R&D is useful for measuring technology-based activities, it is increasingly recognised that this is only one element of the broader concept of innovation . . ." and ". . . firms introduce new products and services onto the market without necessarily performing R&D."
>
> (Scottish Enterprise, 2012:2)

for some inexplicable reasons, the Government of Scotland continues to hold and act on an R&D-centric high-tech focused stance on innovation.

Even amongst some academics, a high-tech perspective of innovation persists. Frenz *et al.* (2004) have tried to explain the higher previous incidence of novel product and process innovation in Scotland despite low R&D per employee, purely from this outlook. They believed that four factors explain this. These are higher proportion of science and engineering graduates as employees, greater use of the science base as a source of knowledge and information, higher propensity to enter into cooperative arrangements for innovation with universities and research organisations and higher proportion of Scottish innovators receiving public policy support for their innovation activity.

As explained previously, much of business innovation in Scotland is in low-tech sectors, which form the core of the Scottish economy. The findings discussed later in this work on Scottish SMEs also show that the innovative small food companies in Scotland do not hire science and engineering graduates, they do not use a science base as a source of information and they do not have cooperative arrangements for innovation with universities and research organisations. Frenz *et al.*'s (2004) explanation thus does not reflect the true nature of innovation in Scotland. The reason for Scotland's appreciable performance in innovation despite its proportionately low R&D is because formal R&D has no role to play in the process of innovation in the majority of low-tech SMEs, of which the Scottish economy is mainly composed.

Conclusions

The Scottish Government pays great attention to monitoring the innovation performance of Scottish businesses and is determined to make Scotland a much more innovative region than it is now. This follows from its view that innovation is a precursor to both competitiveness and growth. Its efforts to achieve this, however, are largely misdirected, as its approach is based on a fallacious notion. It is presumed that innovation is science-led, occurs mostly in high-tech sectors and is caused principally by the investments in R&D. As Scotland has a poor record of business enterprise R&D, the focus is thus to encourage businesses to spend more on R&D and maintain high levels of government R&D to augment low spending by businesses on this count. This, as explained previously, reflects a flawed understanding of the innovation process in general and its nature in the Scottish economy. The fact that in low-tech and traditional sectors, which are the mainstay of the Scottish economy, R&D in the conventional sense has no role must be understood and embedded in policy. There is thus an urgent need to break free from a R&D-centric high-tech view of innovation and search for innovation in the heart of Scottish manufacturing, which is quite innovative despite being low tech.

Notes

1 http://scotland.gov.uk/About/Performance/scotPerforms/indicators/ind1 (accessed 2 August 2013)
2 www.grad.ac.uk (accessed 19 September 2007)
3 www.fsb.org.uk/Member-Survey-2012 (accessed 5 August 2013)

References

European Commission (2004) *Innovation in Europe: Results for the EU, Iceland and Norway Data 1998–2001*, Luxembourg, Sweden: Commission of the European Communities

Frenz, Marion and Oughton, Christine (2005) *Innovation in the UK Regions and Devolved Administrations: A Review of the Literature*, Final Report for the Department of Trade and Industry and the Office of the Deputy Prime Minister

Frenz, Marion, Michie, Jonathan and Oughton, Christine (2004) *Cooperation and Innovation: Evidence from the Community Innovation Survey*, Unpublished paper

HEFCE (2013) Higher Education – Business and Community Interaction Survey, 2011–12, Bristol: Higher Education Funding Council for England

Kleinknecht, A and Reijnen, J O N (1991) More evidence on the undercounting of small firm R&D, Research Policy, 20(6):579–87

Kleinknecht, A (1987) Measuring R&D in small firms: How much are we missing, *Journal of Industrial Economics*, 36(2):253–56

Reid, Alasdair (2012) *A smart, sustainable, nation? A review of Scottish research and innovation policy in the context of the smart specialisation agenda*, Brussels: Technopolis

Santarelli, E and Sterlacchini, A (1990) Innovation, Formal vs Informal R&D, and firm size: Some evidence from Italian manufacturing firms, *Small Business Economics*, 2(3):223–28

Scottish Enterprise (2012) *Innovation in Scotland: Analysis of Community Innovation Survey 2009*, Glasgow: Scottish Enterprise

Scottish Government (2004) *The Framework for Economic Development in Scotland*, Edinburgh: Scottish Government

Scottish Government (2005) *Scottish Business Attitudes to Research, Development and Innovation*, Edinburgh: Scottish Government, DTZ Pieda Consulting

Scottish Government (2006) *Science and Innovation Strategy for Scotland: Consultation Paper*, Edinburgh: Scottish Government

Scottish Government (2007) *The Community Innovation Survey 4: Profiling Scotland's Innovation Performance,* Edinburgh: Scottish Government

Scottish Government (2012a) *Business Enterprise Research and Development Scotland 2011, A National Statistics Publication for Scotland.* Edinburgh: Scottish Government

Scottish Government (2012b) *Businesses in Scotland,* Edinburgh: Scottish Government

Scottish Government (2013) *Chapter 6, Economic Policy Choices in an Independent Scotland,* Edinburgh: Scottish Government

Stead, H (1976) The costs of technological innovation, *Research Policy,* 5(1):2–9

Sterlacchini, Alessandro (1999) do innovative activities matter to small firms in non-R&D-intensive industries? An application to export performance, *Research Policy,* 28(8):819–32

6 Innovation in case study companies

As discussed in Chapter 2, there are two principal perspectives to the analysis of innovation: the determinants perspective and the process perspective. The results of this research are thus presented and analysed from these two perspectives. In the first section, evidence on the nature of the process of innovation in the case study companies is explained; the evidence on presence or otherwise of main determinants of innovation in the case study companies is then discussed in the following section.

Chief components of the innovation process

Idea generation

Idea generation is not a problem for the investigated businesses, driven, as they are, by some exceptionally creative people. None of the respondents said that idea generation was an issue in their enterprises. When asked how often they get new product ideas, the Company A entrepreneur said, "All the time. Continues to come and go. Sometimes it occurs to me, sometimes to chef, sometimes to my father. There are four or five people in the company who continuously (keep on getting new ideas)." The Company D entrepreneur said of her husband, "He is . . . constantly coming out with new ideas." The executive from Company B thought, "If William[1] can get out for a couple of months . . . and just open his mind up, he can come up with a completely new product range."

Idea generation, interestingly, is not a prerogative of the main entrepreneur, although in most cases he or she is the source of most ideas and the very cause of the enterprise's innovativeness. In most organisations, other individuals often supplement the idea-generation task and in one, innovativeness is concentrated in one paid employee, the executive chef. The product development manager of Company B said,

> William is tasked well with being creative as much as possible; he comes up with the ideas of the new flavours and he comes up with packaging

ideas as well, so William has been much of the brains behind (the innovation in the company).

The customer's indirect contribution through adoption of new trends, and in the process bringing pressure on the businesses to create goods reflecting them, is also understood and appreciated by these businesses: "What drives our innovation is actually what consumers want. At the end of the day, it is a consumer who drives any business.". Company C, to prevent a lack of creativity caused by inbreeding, brings in outsiders to reinvigorate the idea-generation process. The company executive said, "Our guys are really busy in the bakery; lots of time with our own products. So, sometimes, we try to get somebody who is really good from outside to show us how it can be done."

There is no evidence of a formal idea-generation process. One respondent said, "Is there a formal process for that? I guess not." And another quipped, "There is no science to it, really."

Most businesses that are investigated here have a close and constant contact with customers. This results in ideas emerging from both ends. The respondent from Company B said,

> He (the chef) might come up with an idea and bring up to people and say, what you think of that? Or we might get a briefing from a customer who would say that we've got a rough idea of what we want to do, and so can you go away and look at it, and so I will say it is roughly 50/50 between the customer-led and our own team leading innovation.

These businesses also continually scan the market and speak to their customers in search of new ideas. This constant feedback fuels their creativity:

> You are watching the market all the time. You are talking to the customer all the time, but also you are looking at your own sales. What is making money? What is not making money? What can you do to better that?

Company F's product development manager said that he gets *new* product ideas from trade journals, food and drinks magazines, customers and suppliers.

The executive from Company B attributed her chef's amazing creativity to this approach: "He has travelled extensively over the years and he's worked in many countries . . . he still travels a lot and eats out and watches all the trends." And "If he can get out for a couple of months, away from the day to day issues and just opens his mind up, he can come up with a completely new product range."

Very rarely, formal market research is undertaken to search for new product ideas. Somehow, the informal process of idea generation seems to work better than formal market research. Company B's product development manager said, "The ones that have been great winners for us (for them), there has been no market research."

Some of them have used innovative methods to generate ideas for the new products. The ice-cream entrepreneur reported,

> In one of the events that we do at adventure centre, the public can come along and we give them milk, cream, sugar and an ice-cream freezer, and we also give them flavours. Strawberry, ginger, chocolate, toffee. If they want, they can bring their own flavours, too, and they can make ice cream, and so we get a huge amount of ideas from the general public on what kind of ice cream they would like, and so we quickly see what is popular.

As mentioned above, some of them rope in outsiders and suppliers. They show ingenuity, however, in not mindlessly churning out the recipes suggested by others. They cleverly change the proposed recipes and mark them with their own style before they go to shelves as their own product: "We take the recipe and we change that to our way. What they do is to tell us a process, but what we do is that we change it."

A persistent urge to keep improving products results in the entrepreneurs looking for ideas on new products that are capable of replacing the existing ones. In Company G, there is a sense of needing to be always looking for new ideas and being entrepreneurial. The notion that you put a product on the market and do not always want to improve it or think of new products is not at all applicable.

The Company A entrepreneur described the process in these words:

> We see what's out there, what's the price and we take the product off the shelf and bring it back here, and we try and evaluate and perceive what (is) the value of it. What is the quality of the product, and based on the quality of the product, we always endeavour to make a product that is better than the original product.

Idea validation

Although developing new food products it is not expensive, innovative companies first go through a process of validating the product idea before proceeding with development . As stated earlier, in some businesses idea validation is a two-stage process, but in most the validation passes through three stages. In the three-stage model, the idea is first internally validated by a small group of people associated with the product development and/or impacted by it, and then it is validated by one or more major customers, usually the grocery superstores.

As stated previously, companies using a two-stage process are smaller companies serving a niche market, such as organic food or farm ice cream, whereas those using a three-stage model have grocery superstores as their biggest and sometimes their only customers. The exceptionally high success rate of new products coming out of these companies is due partly to the participation of grocery chains during the idea-validation process. The market share of supermarkets like Tesco or ASDA, and up-market retaliates such as Marks & Spencer or Waitrose, is substantial, and their endorsement for a new product is quite assuring to small food companies. Sometimes the superstores first approach companies with product ideas, and if what they suggest is within the capability of the small food company it is developed, and it often works. In two-stage validation, the views of friends, relatives and employees usually are sought.

The people involved in idea validation give a cross-functional picture of the innovation process in Scottish food SMEs. As mentioned previously, both the people responsible for product development and those affected by it are involved in the process. Keeping on board those impacted by it from the very beginning helps in understanding and sorting out any teething troubles that may come up when the product is formally commissioned. The product development manager of Company B said, "We've got inputs of marketing and we've got (it) from accounts, production, technical, and development sides." In Company F, once the product development manager gets an idea, he produces a sample himself and then makes a presentation to the production, technical, marketing and finance people. If during this internal presentation the new product idea is accepted, he then shows the sample to buyers, which are either from Waitrose or from Marks & Spencer.

However, when the company is serving a niche market independently, validation happens in two stages and is confined to a small group of close friends, relatives and, sometimes, employees. The logic is, "I just thought that I knew what people wanted. If I like it, my friends liked it (then everybody else would like it too)." In the case of Company G, there is a process of initially testing the entrepreneur's new ideas – either with friends and family or with its own employees and work colleagues – to see if they are worth pursuing further.

Like most parts of innovation in the Scottish food SMEs, idea validation is informal. The product development manager of Company B said, "I'm afraid; we're not very scientific in that regard. It is gut feel." The gut feeling, however, seems to work well, as a large number of people representing a variety of functions are involved in the validation process and look at it from a host of perspectives. She further said,

> We all have a look at it from different sides, as, will that work in the factory, or will we be able to sell that; will we be able to take it off the ground; and around that table if there's a feeling that this is worth a go, then we'll go for it. We won't take it up to the launch stage unless we're convinced that we can do it and we have a market for it.

The validation process, apart from being informal, is also continuous and is woven into the daily company routine. The innovative company personnel seem to be constantly talking innovation. The Company C entrepreneur said,

> We meet at lunchtime every day. If I have an idea or if someone else has an idea, we talk if we can do this or we can do that. To be honest with you, it normally comes not fully developed the first time; you have to make it work. And these guys make it work.

These businesses have a keen sense as to who would best judge the market potential of the product. The ice-cream entrepreneur stated,

> I would judge it very much on myself and my friends. So my test market is very selective. I will just go and talk to my friends . . . . On the food side, too, it is similar, because at the end of the day (the question always is) what food would you like to eat?

The second stage of validation immediately follows the first, and as soon as the idea has been internally validated, the customer is approached with it. The reason for this haste is because most of these companies see their growth potential through the supermarket's sales, and as they use an idea-generation process which is quite simple and available to all interested, they understand that it is not improbable for their competitors to come out with similar products. The issue, therefore, is who approaches the supermarkets with the product idea first. The Company C entrepreneur explained, "If we like the product and if we think it is going to work, we immediately start to talk to the customer to get an idea as to what their reaction is." The Company B's product development manager said, "If you don't go to the customer with new ideas, then somebody else will."

Idea-validation sessions involving a wide spectrum of business functions are sometimes difficult to negotiate, particularly in businesses where the product development manager has the same or lower stature than production people. The product development manager in Company F explained that usually there is a fair amount of resistance to introduce any new product, as it always means significant changes in the scheduling and sequencing of work at the shop floor. Production people do not like to alter the pattern of manufacturing frequently, as it causes a great deal of additional work. Often, genuine objections to new product ideas come in the form of legal restriction on the use of certain ingredients, or on technical difficulties in making the product at the company, given its processing resources.

Idea implementation

The idea-implementation stage of new product development in the investigated businesses is very much concurrent and cross-functional, and there is fair amount of exchange of ideas amongst the people involved. The scenario in Company B is something like this: "The chef is up, the product development guys are there and the packaging guys are there and the production guys are there; everyone's got their cups and saucers and everybody inputs to this (new product) development." In Company A, "The production manager, the managing director, the chairman, the kitchen chef and the technical manager comprise the team." The new product development teams in all but two case study companies have other jobs in the organisation. They work on new product development NPD concurrently with their main job. The entrepreneur from Company A explained,

> We don't have the kind of money that the big boys invest; their NPD people have only an NPD job. Here it is part of ours; we're all near the heart of NPD; it's a part of all the other works that we do.

For implementation, extensive and regular consultation occurs before the final shape is given to the product. These businesses understand the costs of product failure and give credence to the views of all the people, no matter the place they have in the company hierarchy. In Company B, for instance, "everybody inputs to this development, and thereafter we have weekly launch meeting or new-product launch meetings, and everybody can join in and can come to the meetings and raise issues if they have problems with them." Despite this consultation, the basic process remains informal. The Company A entrepreneur explains,

> It is relatively informal, and I say it is relatively informal but it works; you don't need masses of data and research and to hire these research companies to go in and get the product to the market. (We are able to do it because) we know the quality in terms of what we need, and what we lack in comparison. We go far and ahead of the game in the far side of the quality of the products, and the consumer sees the quality side of the products.

The customers, which in many cases are grocery superstores, are involved in the implementation process from the beginning, and the small food companies do not end up wasting resources on unacceptable new products. The product development teams thus remain in constant touch with supermarket representatives throughout the product development process.

Despite the process being informal, and despite people holding other jobs in the company, these companies have evolved an efficient yet intuitive method of converting ideas into successful new products. The success rate of new products in the case study companies is very high, and they are able to put products in the market in a relatively short period.

The implementation stage does not take long in case study companies because in most cases innovation is incremental and so the process is completed within a year at the most, and in most cases in less than 6 months.

Nature of innovation

During this investigation we noticed a significant variation in the innovations that these companies successfully introduced. It included product innovations but also some process and packaging innovations. In product innovation, the underlying idea has been not merely be to be different but also to offer quality that is superior to what is available. The companies' method has been to look at the offerings, contemplate what they lack and then use their expertise to create a superior version. The Company A entrepreneur explained this process vividly:

> We got involved in producing a gluten-free pizza, but it took a lot of time, because the problem with making gluten-free mixes is trying to make comparative products, but we managed to do that because we also have expertise of my father, the senior who also has experience in a wealth of food products, and we developed a high-quality gluten-free pizza which was almost as good as a normal food product, which was quite revolutionary at the time, and the market was very receptive to us because it was packed with quality and so it historically kept us very preoccupied because the (competitor's gluten-free pizzas) are very wet, very dry, very dense, of not very good quality – and so what the market offered was not good enough, and what we developed was an excellent product.

There has also been an emphasis on creating versions that suit the Scottish taste. Company B has "gone over producing something different . . . from the traditional . . . that has a Scottish flavour . . . quite different from what is available in the UK." The Company C entrepreneur who accidentally came across a Japanese pancake machine at a trade fair in Germany, after a long series of trials and errors succeeded in making Scottish pancakes on it, and now has a complete factory dedicated to making pancakes, which are very profitable and are even exported to the US.

Sometimes, innovation occurs just from observing the mundane phenomenon. The Company C entrepreneur, for instance, saw this:

> When you go to the corner shops you buy simple items, something that you want to take home for a reason. So we realised that the big boys (the superstores) are selling four packs, or six or eight, but the people buying from the corner shops do not want to buy such large quantities.

Based on this observation, the company created small-quantity packs exclusively for the corner shops. Innovation here is thus not what the product is or how it is produced. It is in how it is packaged. Again, it is a packaging innovation, not in terms of making it more attractive but just in making it more convenient.

In another, more elaborate effort, Company B introduced new packaging, developed at a cost of £100,000 – a kind of glass jar in which to pack the pâté. The product development manager said, "We put a layer of meat packed in the bottom and a layer of molten cranberries on the top and, things like that where people can see the layers in the jars." There is a constant realisation in these companies that they have to keep on experimenting to expand their markets, and innovation is possible even in products as ordinary as pâté:

> If you produce just purely pâté, only for knifing onto a cracker, then you limit your market, so we've introduced different pâté, kind of, to broaden the appeal, and we've kind of flavoured them so that they appeal to the younger people.

What makes these companies innovative

The investigated businesses owe their ability to innovate to their small size, their flexibility and to the fact that their products are made using methods that are amenable to quick changes. The large businesses using automated processes cannot show the agility needed to alter their products quickly to suit the changing customer needs.

The product development manager in Company B said,

> Producing almost 100 recipes a week, carrying out a very complex operation with innovation and creativity, we have carved for ourselves a niche, and that's what sets us apart from the competition, really. We make small batch runs of specialist products, whereas the large factories have automated equipment, and they just can't do it.

The Company G entrepreneur also said that being small and flexible helped them behave the way they did.

The Company A entrepreneur, in a similar vein, explained:

> In terms of innovation, we have an advantage over the big manufacturers because our ability to change and to change quickly is far greater than of the larger manufacturers, who tend to be heavily geared up and plan equipment for specific products, and to make a change is quite a dramatic problem for them, and hence the way we're settled here, more intensive but we're less mechanized, the ability to innovate our technology or products is far easier for us than for the big manufacturers.

The Company C entrepreneur illustrates this fact with an example:

> We are labour-intensive in terms of many things. Most of the things are handmade. It gives us a lot of flexibility. Morrisons said they like lemon

drizzle but did not want drizzle at the top. They would just like sugar and lemon pieces. If we did not have that flexibility, we cannot do it that easily. Whereas it is a different ball game, down the road (for the large manufacturers).

As mentioned earlier, entrepreneurs and product development executives in innovative companies are driven by a creative urge. The Company C entrepreneur said,

Honestly innovation comes from making something different. How your packaging is? What you do to your products to make it look different? Because everybody makes the same products– everybody has a bakery, and so how different you make your products, that is important; otherwise there is no point.

In case of Company G, it is generally understood that new product development is essential for growth and survival, as food industry has a fair amount of turnover of products due to changing public habits, tastes and preferences and emerging new information on the effects of food on health.

Over the years, these businesses have developed a knack of creating new versions of products by understanding what to change and what to keep constant, and where to look for new ideas without plagiarising. The Company A entrepreneur explained the process of new product development in his organisation in these words:

Say, for instance, pizza. Look at the components of pizza. We know that the heart of the product is the bread base and the pizza sauce which is specifically made for our recipe, and it is stark different from anything else in the market, and that is really the heart of our product. So we, in development, in terms of product innovation, we have to figure out what goes on the top. It can be a type of vegetable or a mix of meat and vegetables. We tend to try not to copy anybody in any of our own creations in terms of products. So sometimes it is ham and potato, sometimes peach and sometimes mixed peppers and onions. . . .Whatever we do, we do it in a way that offers quality. So people associate our brand with quality, and the innovation comes from the chef's lair in terms of new ideas presented to the market. That is the key to how we innovate. We have a look at loads of shelves and see what's there, but we don't copy others. We could never do that. We just take bits and pieces of ideas from different products, stick them together in a totally different way and present it as a totally new concept.

A combination of factors thus seems to be at work. On the demand side a relentless pressure from the supermarkets and up-market grocery retailers, driven by an increasingly variety-based competition to offer new products and new packaging reflecting the changing tastes and preferences of consumer, and on the supply side the creative urge of some exceptionally gifted people, their long experience in the food industry and the flexibility and speed of their organisations to develop and deliver new goods in quick time. The Company C entrepreneur tries to capture the idea in these words:

> I have been in the bakery industry for over 5 years. Thomas has been for years and years, so has Colin. Phil has been there for a long time. You tend to find that they (new products) come around in circles, and the trick is to go and act at the right time in circle. The superstores almost preempt us. They are always looking for something different. We take to the multiple something that is new . . . pancake would be great, and the reaction of superstores is yes, yes it seems good, but we are talking about packaging as well. All these things, everything contributes to innovation. It is very difficult to pin down.

How the grocery superstores are driving innovation

The role of grocery superstores – which include superstores such as Tesco and ASDA, and high-end retailers like Marks & Spencer and Waitrose – in driving innovation in the Scottish food SMEs is noticeable from this investigation.

All investigated businesses, except one, supply mainly to grocery superstores. For instance, Company G's main market is Tesco, and business had grown so much that they have had to get some manufacturing done by a subcontractor in Wales. Company F sells largely to large buyers like Marks & Spencer and Waitrose. It also has products being sold to superstores such as Sainsbury and Tesco, although sales to superstores are a smaller percentage. Company C was previously predominantly a corner-shop supplier; it now supplies to ASDA, Morrisons, Aldi, Sainsbury and Waitrose.

As depicted in Figure 6.1, remarkable complementary roles are played by the innovative small food companies on the supply side, and supermarkets and large retailers on the demand side are driving the food sector innovation in Scotland.

This complementariness is based on mutual need. Supermarkets are reaching the limits of price-based competition. They are also restrained by law in increasing the number and size of their outlets. For them, competition is therefore becoming increasingly variety-based. They want to show their customers that they have what their rivals do not have. They are therefore in a perennial search for new products

Small companies in the Scottish food industry, on the other hand, realise that the road to fast growth is through the grocery superstores' shelves, which offer significant market opportunity to any small company due to their huge customer base. It is, however, not easy to break into a large chain like Waitrose or Marks & Spencer, as they would not discontinue an

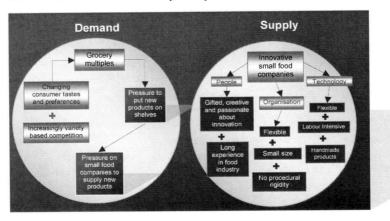

Figure 6.1 Demand and supply of new food products

incumbent supplier unless it does something terribly wrong, and existing suppliers would not do such a thing, as it would be the virtual end for them. The Company D entrepreneur said,

> We have been trying for years to get into Waitrose. And they are a great company to supply to, but they always say that we think your ice cream is wonderful but we have got a really good relationship with our existing ice-cream supplier and they haven't put a foot wrong.

Once a company succeeds in entering the fold of a retailer such as Waitrose, however, it gets good support. Company B's product development manager said,

> What we've got in terms of support from Waitrose (is so great) that we've got absolutely no bad word to say about them. I don't think that any company has got a bad word to say about them. They'll try your new product. They'll give you time to make it work. They're loyal.

As mentioned earlier, not only is it difficult for a small food company to break into supermarkets, it is also virtually impossible if the small food company is not innovative. It is almost forced upon small food companies to be innovative if they wish to supply to supermarkets. A company executive said,

> The way to do it with supermarkets is that if you want to break into them, (then) if you get them something, even the same product, even a better quality, even at better price, you won't win the business. They will not take anything from you, which they are getting from their existing

suppliers. So you have to think of something new. A lot of our innovative thinking came from that.

It is enough to be innovative to enter the supermarkets, but you have to continue to innovate if you wish to grow. Company B's product development manager said,

> I suppose they are more demanding. If they want something, then they'll say, this is where were going, and if you don't want to come along then we'll go elsewhere. So we've invested heavily in this factory to keep up with Waitrose, but it paid off. And we've got over a million pounds worth of sales to them this year and over £1.8 million worth of sales in Tesco. So any investment that we've made, nearly half of that has worked for what we can say is a very demanding customer.

The Company C entrepreneur made the same point: "The superstores almost preempt us. They are always looking for something different."

Supermarkets, however, are not passively waiting for innovative companies to approach them. They look proactively for innovators. ASDA, for instance, organises and judges contests and then encourages the winners to supply to it.

Another important point, as indicated in Chapter 4, is that many noninnovative food companies whose products competed directly with supermarkets have been forced to close down due to their inability to match the low prices of the supermarkets. Innovate or perish is therefore the message that the increasing stranglehold of supermarkets on the British grocery trade implies for small food companies, in Scotland and elsewhere.

Types of innovation

Two of the previous Community Innovation Surveys (European Commission, 2004 and Scottish Government, 2007) show that a high proportion of Scottish enterprises are novel-product innovators. However, this changed later, and the Community Innovation Surveys' proportion of Scottish enterprises that are novel product innovators dropped to 30% and 39% for 2005 and 2009, respectively. This investigation of innovation in the Scottish food SMEs shows that the case studies companies did not create any radically different products.

There is some evidence of imitation in this industry. The recurrent theme, however, is that of incremental innovation. The Company C entrepreneur said, "We make it a little bit different," and the Company E entrepreneur stated, "If you think in terms of completely new products, then I have not done that before. It is always a variation in theme." Some of the businesses involved, however, do not call this practice incremental innovation; they use the phrase 'range change'. Company B's product development manager explained: "Simple range change ideas, when, say, a new ingredient has come onto the market– say Australian bush herbs, or something like that– that's a range change one. This will happen three or four times a year." We may call it supply-side incremental change. The demand-side incremental change occurs when an attempt is made to create varieties to suit changing customer tastes.

As stated above, some people in the industry use a distinct jargon to describe the prevalent incremental innovation practices. A *range change* (also called 'line extensions' by some) involves changing only some ingredients in a product that is otherwise identical to the previously made product; a *recipe change* involves making an altogether new recipe, previously not a part of company's product range. This recipe then may undergo several range changes over its life. Ultimate in the league is the *format change,* which may involve major changes in packaging or processing. The highest level of innovation in the industry is thus, not radical, a product or a process which is altogether different from the present one. The highest level of innovation here is one that involves a significant alteration in the production or in packaging methods. The format change thus is a combination of comparatively more substantial product and process innovation.

Healthy foods

The International Food Information Council Foundation (IFICF) ascribes the growing interest in functional foods to consumers' realisation of the impact of diet on health along with 'rapid advances in science and technology, increasing health-care costs, changes in food laws, aging population, and rising interest in attaining wellness through diet'(IFICF, 2011: 1). Functional, healthier and organic foods apparently are the obvious choice for food companies wishing to create innovative new products. The phenomenal growth of Finnish food companies is attributed to their focused search for functional foods.

Amongst the case study companies, however, only one is a health-food company which specialises in organic foods. This company employs a 'nutrition expert', but the entrepreneur is also quite conversant with what is considered healthy food. (For example, she said that many of the health drinks with 'friendly bacteria' were useless because most of would not have survived in the product during its shelf life.) The overall market target for this company is 'healthy food', even to the extent of baby food, and the entrepreneur was clearly aware of how demand was steadily rising and also how at particular times of the year – after Christmas, for example – the demand for their products (and also for general diet products) shows a marked increase.

In the rest of the case study companies, however, healthy foods are not at the core of the innovation process. Company A, for instance, is developing foods that are healthy because of the company's product development history and not as a consequence of healthy-eating trends. Its innovative effort happens to be creating healthy products by coincidence rather than by design. The entrepreneur explained,

> What we have isn't (the result of) a conscious decision taken by us, we naturally come from a restaurant background and so we developed products that are far more wholesome and nutritional and use less additives and artificial ingredients than some of the big manufacturers, so that in itself are healthy in their own right but not by a conscious effort.

This company's biggest innovation has been a gluten-free pizza, and so they obviously are influenced by the health effects of foods and have avoided any dubious substances when creating new products. The entrepreneur, speaking of such additives, said, "We don't use any of that in our flour base, we use wholesome and (we try) to have a chemical-free product, and we have always done it."

However, as dietary trends influence the sale of meals more than the sale of finished food products, the impact on Company A has been minimal. The entrepreneur explained:

> We do not have big enough market for our meals and our brands that could show the impact of change in dietary requirement. So it is a grey area for us. . . . No, I don't think Atkins has made any impact on us at all.

It is noteworthy that there is an absence of any conscious and concerned effort in case study companies to create goods that take advantage of the public's concern about the health impact of diet. The effort is to create goods that do not violate such concerns. These concerns, however, are peripheral to new product development processes.

Food companies, from a market perspective, divide their products in two broad categories: those that people buy for their nutritional needs and those that they buy as indulgences. The former are bought on a daily basis and the latter only occasionally. There seems to be an overwhelming consensus that there is no need to make the indulgences, which people buy for taste, healthy. It is believed that trying to make them healthy would compromise their taste and would jeopardise the very reason that people buy them. Innovation in case study companies, therefore, focuses more on indulgences rather than on nutritional foods. As Company B's product development manager explained,

> Some of them are (healthy) and some of them aren't. We do vegetarian products, and we do weight watchers ones and they are healthy, but probably the majority of them are more indulgent ones, and it's not something that you have daily. It's more of a special occasion one.

Some companies did, in fact, try to take the healthy food route early on but now believe that it was a mistake, particularly as their products are sold mainly in Scotland. The Company D entrepreneur said,

> We also tried our organic range because we have an organic farm. We launched the organic range in 1999, and we had thought that by this time everything that we will be doing would be organic. The information that we got at that time was that the organics were growing exponentially up. We were the second organic ice-cream company in the whole of UK. So we were the early starters but now we know that Scotland has not got the income where people can afford it. Scotland has not got the pollution where people would feel that they must buy organic and we (the Scottish people) are not as trendy or trendsetters, and so all the information that we had that organic were going skywards wasn't true for Scotland. Supermarkets said you test market it for Scotland. We tried it and it did not work, and now it sells, the vast majority of it, only in London in independent stores.

The Company C entrepreneur narrated a similar story but highlighted an important fact. Supermarkets that are responsible for driving innovation in this sector do not favour healthy foods, which are poor sellers. He stated,

> We manufactured the first pancake with less than 3% fat, high fruit content, good and healthy . . . (but) every one of our superstores said we were wasting our time . . . dealers want chocolates full of fat, custard full of fat, everything full of fat; even salad, full of fat. Everything has (to have) fat in it. That is what they want. (There are) two reasons for that, I think, . . . One is that if someone is going to buy a pack of pancake as an indulgence, they are not going to buy them three times a day. They are going to buy twice a week or may be once a week. I think if you are selling something, which is not an everyday food, sandwiches and like (then there is no problem if it has high fat). (Names a superstore) has a system through which they have found out that people who buy Scottish cake, Irn Bru, Square Sausage, Mars Bars and things like that, they don't buy low-fat products and so (they think), why to worry, and that, to be honest, is superstores' philosophy. They all know that and are very, very shrewd. They do not bother about low fat, low sugar in things, which people buy as indulgence. We have been told by (names a superstore) that your attempt to make low-fat, low-sugar cakes is commendable, but we will not take them because people will not buy them, they taste horrible. . . . Even the weight watchers think that if you are not going to buy it every day, why not buy a proper cake and enjoy it.

Packaging

In the food industry, packaging is an integral part of the product. In the food service sector, the quality of a restaurant dish is reflected both in its taste as well as in its presentation. Similarly, the quality of food on a supermarket shelf is judged first by its packaging and then by its taste. Nature has taught humans that delicious things to eat come in attractive shapes, colours and fragrances, and so the seasoned food developers have learnt to present their creations in attractive designs and shapes. This makes packaging an essential part of the product, and innovative food companies spend considerable time in creatively packaging their products to increase saleability.

The other relevant issue is that when the customer unpacks the food at home the food's contents must come out the same way it was assembled People do not like the idea of a cake's crumbled icing mixed with the main body of the cake. The Company C entrepreneur explained: "We have to deal with a whole lot of cake packaging, which took a lot of time. We had to redesign it. And it is designed so good that even if you turn it upside down it won't move."

The investigated businesses spoke of packaging innovation as a part of product innovation. As soon as a new food is created, work begins to create packaging that gives maximum leverage to it as a new food, and so new food ideas and new packaging ideas emerge quite intertwined. Sometimes packaging innovation stands alone, and without making any changes in the product itself, just through creative packaging, the market is expanded. The Company C entrepreneur explained:

> The big boys are selling four packs, or six or eight packs, but the people buying from corner shops do not want to buy such large quantities. By creating two packs of cakes and things like that, a person can go and buy instead of four packs one . . . we have been successful.

Pricing strategy

Case study companies adopt a two-pronged pricing strategy: relatively low prices for supermarkets and high prices for up-market retailers. This is obviously not a blanket strategy and simplistic price discrimination, offering the same stuff with cosmetic variations to these two groups of retailers. Customer involvement from the beginning of product development rules out such a strategy. As a company executive put it, "another basic issue with a Marks & Spencer cake would be that commercially we cannot do it at the price ASDA or Tesco are asking us to do it."

From the idea-generation stage the product developers know whether the product is destined for supermarkets or going up-market. Their long experience in food development tells them early on, given the ingredients and the level of processing involved, what range the costs would ultimately balance and what kind of price would be feasible, and given the price, who the customer might be. Another significant issue here is that even those products that would end up at price-conscious supermarket's shelves are amongst supermarket's more expensive offerings. Two things influence this. Innovation does not come cheap, and as mentioned earlier, supermarkets encouraging food companies to develop new products are trying to address the issue of variety and not price in terms of their competition strategy. The food companies, on the other hand, know that innovation in high-margin varieties is more rewarding and worth the effort. Many of them are following a conscious strategy of creating more luxuriant versions of the existing products. High margins and high prices are consistent with this strategy. As the product development manager in Company B put it,

> We always thought that we had only to concentrate on natural flavours, on luxurious flavours . . . (and so I think) we could only go up. I did not think we could go down. If we try to go to the low market . . . (we will not make money).

Similarly, Company F has a smaller percentage of products being sold to superstores such as Sainsbury and Tesco, mainly because its products are a high-margin, expensive variety, which do not fit well with the superstores low-price strategies. The product development manager believes that it is not possible to visualise cheap seafood, particularly in his line of products, as the basic ingredient in many cases is very expensive. He does not seem to bother about low acceptability of his product on the supermarket shelves, as he gets enough business from up-market retailers like Marks & Spencer and Waitrose.

Quality

The case study companies do not merely develop new products; they develop high-quality new products, and that quality need is embedded in their process of innovation. The investigated product developers have perfected a process that ensures that their new products are of high quality, consistent with their name and image. The Company A entrepreneur explains:

> Motivation for me is . . . make sure that we make a product that's a value for our name and our brand, and (we) keep coming up with products that people enjoy. . . . I like it. . . . I get a kick when I see (customers') reactions and get their feedback, and how the markets have been dragged into the gutter by poor products over the decades and how we can get over that.

To get the quality right, these companies are willing to go the extra mile. For instance, Company G subcontracted some manufacturing in Wales. The entrepreneur seemed almost regretful about having to do this outside of Scotland but was very fussy about quality, and because only this company in Wales seemed to be able to complete the manufacturing the way they wanted it done, they subcontracted against their patriotic instincts. Company C's entrepreneur put it succinctly : "It is that everybody does it but we do it better."

This is why the validation stage is so important for these food companies. Both the three-stage and the two-stage validation companies make sure that quality that is not just acceptable but irresistible to the customer is the end result. One can say that strategically these companies are intentionally searching for more luxuriant and higher quality products that are capable of being positioned at the higher end of the value chain. This allows them to charge a high price, making innovation both rewarding and profitable. Charging a high price, however, is not possible through spurious quality, and so genuine high quality becomes an integral part of the product development strategy. At the same time, as the Scottish people in general are not very conscious of the health effects of diet, this strategy does not take the direction of organic or functional foods, and so most food companies are focused on indulgences, which is consistent with their high-price, high-margins, low-volume business model.

The innovation process in the Scottish food SMEs: A summary

From vague ideas to fully formed new products, the process of innovation in the case study companies passes through three distinct phases. These constitute generation, validation and implementation of new product ideas.

The seeds of innovation, in the form of fuzzy product ideas, sprout in an enterprise from a variety of sources, from within and from outside. The principal entrepreneur is usually the most prolific generator of new product ideas. In many enterprises, however, other individuals, very often members of the product development teams, demonstrate creativity in equal measures. At the other end, customers, if they are grocery superstores, prompted by their own market research that keeps a tab on consumers and competitors, present these companies with new ideas to pursue. There is no evidence of any formal processes here, but there is ample indication of a combination of 'reaching out' to pluck ideas from outside as well as 'churning' them internally. Most remarkable is an absence of a 'not invented here' attitude. These businesses are willing to try ideas without being fussy about their source. This sometimes adds a certain element of imitation to their product development efforts. As exceptionally creative, however, as the individuals at the helm of product development process in these enterprises are, they are always able to put their own stamp on the ideas so borrowed.

Once a product idea has been identified as worth pursuing, it goes through a process of validation. There are two stages of validation. Validation of market potential comes first. The product is made in very small quantities, in an experimental way, akin to the production of prototypes in scientific research. Then, as a prototype is tested in a lab to establish a scientific principle, the product is tested 'literally' by a group of individuals that will give their verdict on how they find the product as an edible food. The notion behind such 'test marketing' is that a group that includes 'you, your friends, your employees and your relatives' is a reasonably representative sample of the food market, and if this group likes a new product in significant numbers, it has potential. The second phase is the validation of production feasibility. Here the product development team, along with the manufacturing, finance, design, packaging and marketing personnel, assess the capacity of the enterprise to produce it in the quantities in which it will likely sell.

In the three-stage validation, the first two stages occur more or less as described previously, and then the product is further validated by one or more major customers, usually the grocery superstores. The three-stage validation has the benefit of receiving a further and crucial stamp of approval, which, in essence, reinforces the first-stage validation of the market potential of the product.

Two things seem to separate the two-phase validation companies from the three-phase companies: the size of enterprise and the target market. Companies using two-stage validation are smaller companies serving a niche market that usually do not need significant changes in existing manufacturing to produce the new product. Those using three-stage validation are slightly larger, principally supply to the grocery superstores and often need some changes in manufacturing to create new goods. It is interesting to understand why the enterprises serving niche markets do not need many changes in manufacturing to create new products, whereas those serving the superstores need them more often. Niche markets, by their very nature, absorb very narrowly defined products. The new products in a niche market are usually not dramatically different from a company's existing products because such a difference may not allow them to serve the same niche. Grocery superstores, on the other hand, sell a wide variety of foods, and so new products destined towards superstores can be very different from the existing products and therefore may need significant changes in the production processes to manufacture them.

Idea validation, though largely informal, works well because a large number of people, representing a variety of internal functions (as well as the grocery superstores' representatives, in the three-stage version) interact continuously, closely scrutinising the potential products from many points of view. The process is akin to the cubist perspective in painting, explained by Hughes (1980:20):

> Picasso and Braque wanted to represent the fact that our knowledge of an object is made up of all possible views of it: top, sides, front, back. They wanted to compress this inspection, which takes time, into one moment, one synthesised view.

In the implementation stage of new product development, the new product is produced in market-scale quantities. Implementation is concurrent in the sense that although the product has been launched, it is still being developed. The product development team is actively absorbing the early market response and effecting changes both in the content of the product and the way it is produced. It is also cross-functional in the sense that production personnel are also involved as the product, although still experimental in a way, is being produced for the real market. Implementation involves intensive and continuous consultation amongst all stakeholders, as new challenges surface and are addressed. The success rate of new products in the case study companies is very high, and they are able to put products in the market in a relatively short period. One of the reasons for such success, despite little or no market research, is that apart from an informal and yet robust validation, these companies do not have to get it right the first time. As the product is a food item, bought in small quantities on a daily basis, the companies continue to monitor customer reactions after the launch and are able to make changes for some time, even as it is being produced, packed and put on the shelves. Early customer reactions continue to influence product changes until they get it right. (Such flexibility, however, is circumscribed by stringent standardisation norms manifested in HACCP and by the fact that some superstores do not allow changes in the product after it has been put on the shelves). Despite this trial-and-error approach, implementation does not take long in small food companies in Scotland, reflecting high agility of these enterprises in reading the signals that they receive from the market and acting upon them. The process from ideas to final products is completed within a year at the most, and in many cases in less than 6 months.

Determinants of innovation

The internal strategic determinants of innovation identified by previous research and discussed in Chapter 2 include market orientation, learning processes, technology policy, participation in cooperative networks, managerial efficiency, adequacy of financial and human resources, the role of innovative people and the age as well as size of the enterprise. Evidence of these in the case study companies is analysed below.

Market orientation: Within-case analysis

The level of market orientation of a firm is postulated to be based on the integration of customers into the product innovation processes, the ability to explore and reach potential markets, the fit between market needs and the firm's resources, product planning from inception, targeting the international market, the span of market experience, understanding of customer needs and user circumstances, competition analysis, speed and flexibility, market research, market tests and deployment of user feedback to modify an innovation (Edgett & Parkinson, 1994; Storey & Easingwood, 1996; Soderquist *et al.*, 1997; Heydebreck, 1997; De Brentani, 2001 and Lindman, 2002). From the analysis of information from the case study companies, the following indicators of market orientation are identified.

Company A reflects an ability to explore and reach potential markets; it tries to attain a good fit between market needs and the firm's resources, undertakes competition analysis, has a long span of market experience (35 years) and exhibits a good understanding of customer needs and user circumstances. Although it did not target the international market at the time of the investigation, it does it now. The company, however, does not carry out market research or undertake market tests. The absence of these indicators of market orientation does not necessarily mean that the company is less market-oriented. It only shows the nature of its market orientation.

Company B demonstrates integration of customers into the product innovation processes, an ability to explore and reach potential markets, a fit between market needs and the firm's resources, product planning from inception, a long span of market experience, an understanding of customer needs and user circumstances and high speed and flexibility in new product development as well as informal market research. There is, however, no evidence of the targeting of international markets, the use of competition analysis, or the use of market tests. The reason for absence of the last two indicators is understandable. Having developed an enduring relationship with a major food retailer, the company has made itself fairly safe from the actions of its competitors. Another reason for its lack of interest in competition analysis is that in its niche, it is very well placed in the UK. Although it is a small company, in the pâté market it is considered the market leader. The reason for the nonuse of market tests appears to be because it sells its products through large grocery multiples and it does not need to depend on such tests which are crucial to companies selling directly to final consumer.

Company D is a highly market-oriented enterprise, and it exhibits most indicators of market orientation, except for targeting the international market and deploying user feedback to modify an innovation.

The indicators of market orientation exhibited by Company E are ability to explore and reach potential markets, fit between market needs and the firm's resources, targeting the international market, long span of market experience, understanding of customer needs and user circumstances, use of competition analysis, high speed and flexibility and use of market tests. The indicators on which it has not shown sufficient evidence are the integration of customers into the product innovation processes, product planning from inception, market research and the deployment of user feedback to modify an innovation.

Company F's high market orientation is evident in its integration of customers into product innovation processes, its ability to explore and reach potential markets, a good fit between market needs and the firm's resources, product planning from inception, a long span of market experience, an understanding of customer needs and user circumstances and deployment of user feedback to modify an innovation. Company F also uses rudimentary market research. The company, however, does not carry out competitor analysis, it does not use market tests nor has it targeted the international market.

Company G has a reasonably high market orientation. It demonstrates an ability to explore and reach potential markets, has a moderate span of market experience, uses competition analysis, high speed and flexibility in product development and deployment of user feedback to modify an innovation.

Market orientation: Cross-case analysis

Company analysis

Out of 12 indicators of market orientation considered in this research, the case study companies show evidence on an average of eight indicators. We can thus say that these companies are highly market-orientated. Amongst these companies, Company D is the most market-orientated, as it shows evidence on nine indicators. Companies A, B, and E exhibit presence of eight indicators, and Companies C and F show evidence on seven of them. Company G is the least market-oriented of all case study companies.

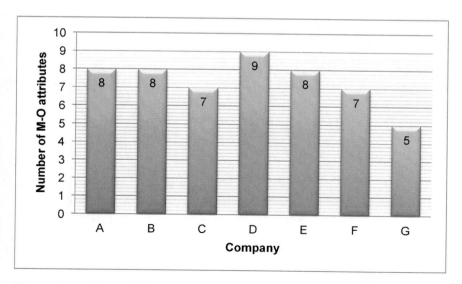

Figure 6.2 Market orientation in case study companies

Indicator analysis

The ability to explore and reach potential markets is visible in all seven case study companies. Also, they all show a long span of market experience, the minimum being 9 years. Fit between market needs and the firm's resources, understanding of customer needs and user circumstances and speed and flexibility in new product development is shown by six of them. Relatively less frequent are product planning from inception, competition analysis and market research. The least observed indicators of market orientation are targeting the international market, use of market tests and deployment of user feedback to modify an innovation.

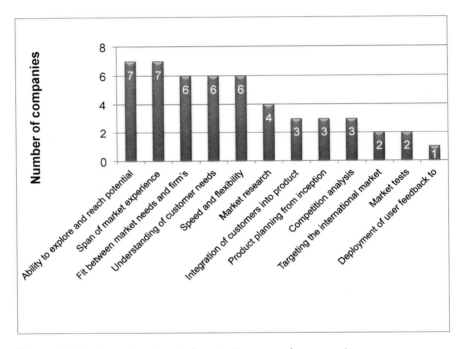

Figure 6.3 Market-orientation indicators in case study companies

Learning processes: Within-case analysis

Research in the field identifies innovation-influencing learning processes in a firm as, knowledge formation to drive innovation strategically, the fostering of creativity, the ability to spot opportunities for innovation, an appreciation of and need for absorbing new ideas and continuous learning (Stata, 1989; Angle, 1989; Hurley & Hult, 1998 and Morgan *et al.*, 1998). The evidence of various indicators of learning processes in the seven investigated enterprises follows:

Company A's learning processes are evident in knowledge formation to drive innovation strategically, the ability to spot opportunities for innovation, an appreciation of and need for absorbing new ideas and continuous learning. The only indicator of which there is little evidence is fostering creativity. The present Managing Director (MD) and his septuagenarian father both have been very creative. They do not, however, seem to have tried to foster creativity in their staff. This, in the longer term, may create problems for the enterprise.

Learning processes at Company B are underpinned by the unusual creativity of its executive chef. There is overwhelming appreciation of his creative genius and genuine respect for his ideas. He also has a unique method to generate ideas and has a role in implementing them as well. There is no attempt, however, to try to pass on his methods to other individuals in the organisation, which could prove costly if he were to leave the organisation.

Company C is the most rounded-learning organisation for innovation. It presents evidence on all five indicators of innovation-influencing learning processes.

Company D's learning processes are evident in knowledge formation to drive innovation strategically, the ability to spot opportunities for innovation, an appreciation of and need for absorbing new ideas and continuous learning. Here, too, the only indicator of which there is little evidence is fostering creativity. Entrepreneurs behind the company are a very committed couple, dedicated to a host of causes, principally to sustainable innovation. The creativity of the husband and the pragmatism of the wife complement the innovative processes ideally. They seem to have not, however, tried to foster creativity in their staff, which does not bode well for long-run sustainability of innovation in the enterprise.

Company E's learning processes are evident in the ability to spot opportunities for innovation and in continuous learning. There is not much evidence of knowledge formation to drive innovation strategically, an appreciation of and need for absorbing new ideas and for fostering creativity. The enterprise thus demonstrates limited learning processes to drive innovation. The impact of this on the innovation process is reflected in company's focus on incremental innovation.

Company F shows evidence of fostering creativity, an ability to spot opportunities for innovation, an appreciation of and need for absorbing new ideas and of continuous learning. Company F is thus a well-rounded learning organisation. The only indictor not exhibited by Company F is knowledge formation to drive innovation strategically.

The learning processes visible in the behaviour of Company G comprise knowledge formation to drive innovation strategically, the fostering of creativity and continuous learning.

Learning processes: Cross-case analysis

Company analysis

Showing proof on all the indicators of learning processes, Company C is the most learning organisation amongst the case study companies. Companies

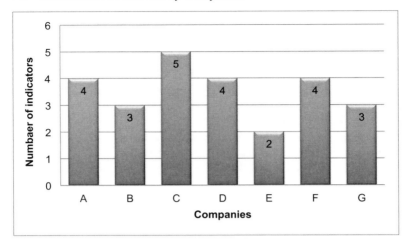

Figure 6.4 Learning processes in the case study companies

A, D and F emerge as reasonably good learning companies. Companies B and G are moderate learning organisations. Company E, however, shows more need for improvement on this count than any other case study company.

Indicator analysis

The most found indicators of learning processes in the investigated enterprises are the ability to spot opportunities for innovation and continuous learning. These indicators can be seen in six case study companies. Also evident are knowledge formation to drive innovation strategically, the appreciation of and need for absorbing new ideas and fostering creativity.

As discussed above, in three of the case study companies some very creative individuals are spearheading innovation. However, there is no attempt to foster creativity in other members of staff, which is not a good sign, because if these individuals were to leave these companies, the organisational innovative processes may not continue.

Technology policy: Within-case analysis

Previous research in the field identifies the presence of an innovation-determining technology policy in a firm based on the development of new ideas, products and processes, strong R&D orientation, active search for new technological knowledge, product uniqueness, products with technological newness, products with large application scope and active acquisition of new technologies (Cooper, 1984, 1994 and Lindman, 2002).

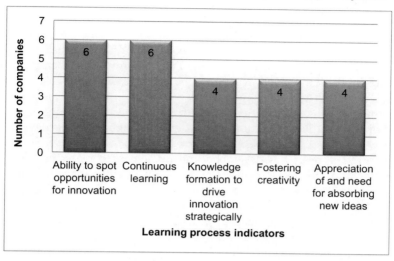

Figure 6.5 Incidence of indicators of learning processes in the case study companies

Company A has been constantly trying to develop new ideas, products and processes. Although its basic product, pizza, provides a limited scope for innovation, it has made it a quest to innovate its pizza as much as it can. In the process, it has developed many unique products, such as gluten-free pizza, corn pizza and microwave pizza. Its microwave pizza can be considered a product with technological newness. The company has also successfully created many derivatives of its gluten-free pizza. Company A, at the time of this investigation, had reached a development threshold where because of growing demand of its products, it was finding it difficult to continue to use its labour-intensive techniques. It was searching for technologies whereby it could mechanise its production without losing the advantage of quality of its handmade products.

At Company B, continuous development of ideas, products and processes is almost a way of life. Its executive chef, endowed with exceptional creativity, travels extensively in search of new ideas. These ideas are then developed with enthusiasm and commitment by the company. Company B is very much a one-product business. It has, however, become a market leader in the UK in its segment of food market by creating its own unique range. In order to create a packaging of its own type, the company invested £100,000 in a new technology to pack its pâté in a glass jar, which the product development executive showed with pride. Company B has tried steadfastly to broaden the appeal of its product and has tried strategically to expand its application scope.

Acquiring a Japanese pancake-making machine from a trade fair in Germany and then working tirelessly to make Scottish pancakes on it is an example of both the development of new products and an active acquisition of new technology by Company C. Company C takes technical advice actively from its suppliers to know what new products can be developed using the ingredients that they supply. There is always an attempt to try to gain technical knowledge, which can be productively used given the company's resources and prior knowledge.

Company D has transformed itself from a subsistence farm into a showcase of sustainable innovation and growth through a tireless development of new ideas and products. Around the broad themes of ice cream and an adventure centre, it has developed and implemented many ideas, such as Banoffee and Heather-Cream ice creams and organic as well as fair-trade ice creams. It constantly tries to improve its technology base. Entrepreneurs travel regularly to distant destinations in search of new technology.

Company E has positioned itself as an exporter of characteristic Scottish foods to North America and locally to the Scottish gift trade. It has come a long way to reach this point. On the way, it has experimented and developed a very diverse mix of food and drinks products. Not all of them have been successful, and the enterprise took some time to realise its final destination. It has also created fresh product designs, one of which it has copyrighted.

Company F, like the rest of the case study companies, has a systematic approach to develop new ideas and products. Once the product development executive gets an idea, he produces a sample and then makes a presentation to the production, technical, marketing and finance people. From the feedback that he receives, he modifies the sample and then discusses it with representatives of up-market grocery chains, who are his main customers. Company F is a part of a group which has incorporated innovation into its main policy and which has a team of five powerful individuals at the group headquarters that ensure that all companies in the group continue to remain innovative and develop new products on a regular basis.

The investigation of Company G shows a need to be constantly looking for new ideas and being entrepreneurial. The notion that you put a product on the market and do not always want to improve it or think of new products just is not at all applicable to it. The entrepreneur said the company often has as many as six new products being developed at the same time. Company employees also actively search for new technological knowledge. For that purpose, read and travel extensively in search of new knowledge in their field. At the time of interview, one of the founders of the organisation was going to Finland for that purpose. Most of Company G's products are unique, essentially because there are not many companies making organic ready meals and soups, and so the very nature of the market niche that this company was set up to exploit makes its products unique. During the interview, the entrepreneur gave some examples of products for which there were in fact no other competitors because there were no other similar products. One such product is a health drink that does not contain lactose.

Technology policy: Cross-case analysis

Company analysis

In relative terms, the case study companies have not done as well in terms of demonstrating evidence of innovation influencing technology policy as they have in terms of other determinants. The reason for this is not difficult to surmise. These are not high-tech enterprises and so technology policy is not a major driver of innovation here.

Figure 6.6 shows that Company A has a reasonable record of innovation influencing technology policy with five (out of seven) indicators. Companies B, with four indicators, and Companies C, D and G, with three each, and company F and E with only two have relatively poor technology policy evidence.

Indicator analysis

All investigated enterprises exhibit evidence on the development of new ideas, products and processes, and it is only to be expected: The subject of this investigation is innovation and new product development. These organisations were picked because of their known success in the development of new products. As expected, the results show all of these companies developing new products and/or processes.

The noteworthy fact is that four investigated enterprises have developed unique products, which confirm them as innovative companies. On the remaining indicators, however, these organisations have not done so well in

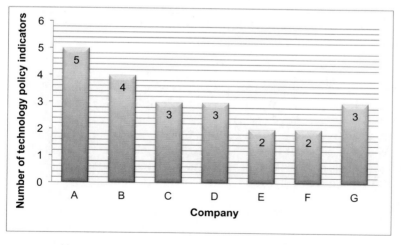

Figure 6.6 Technology policy indicators in the case study companies

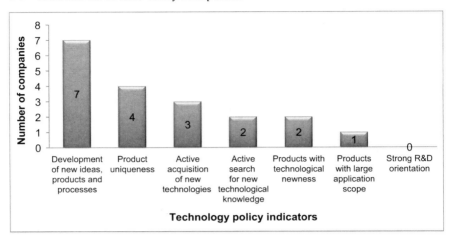

Figure 6.7 Incidence of technology policy indicators in the case study companies

terms of innovation influencing technology policy. For example, the active acquisition of new technologies is evident only in three enterprises, and an active search for new technological knowledge and products with technological newness are exhibited by only two.

Products with large a application scope are developed by only one company. This implies that most of these enterprises are active in strong niche markets and have not attempted to go beyond these niches. Most significantly, this investigation reveals that not one of the seven investigated enterprises have strong R&D orientation. This corroborates the major conclusion of this research that innovation in the Scottish food industry is low tech and raises questions on the relevance of the R&D-centric innovation policy of the Scottish Government.

Cooperation and networking: Within-case analysis

Company A collaborates with other Scottish food companies. The collaboration, however, is not in new product development but in marketing their products. As stated earlier, Company A has a very successful product development regime and feels no need to network with other companies for innovation. For small enterprises, marketing is always a challenge. Company A, which supplies to superstores to a limited extent and therefore needs to expand its market, has thus joined a network of Scottish food companies for jointly marketing its produce.

Company B has been an active participant in a long tradition of collaboration within the Scottish food and drinks industry. Collaboration with other companies, however, is need-based and often an on/off affair. It more regularly collaborates with its major customer, Waitrose, and less frequently with other food companies and suppliers. Networking in the case of Company B is shaped more by complementariness rather than the need for it to work with competitors for mutual benefit. Company B has had support from Scottish Enterprise as well.

Company C cooperates with its suppliers for product development. Company C, however, ensures that when it eventually develops a product based on such a collaboration the other enterprises are not able to copy the product. Company C does not cooperate with their competitors in the bakery industry.

Company D is part of a cluster of Scottish ice-cream makers. The entrepreneur, however, did not seem very enthusiastic about group participation. There is no evidence of collaboration in product development but in acquisition of new equipment. Company D receives regular support from Scottish Enterprise.

Company E is not involved in any cooperation or networking with other food companies. The entrepreneur stated that the organisation hires consultants to complete tasks it cannot perform rather than seek advice or support from other food entrepreneurs. Company E has been receiving support from Scottish Enterprise for new product development, although the entrepreneur believes support used to be much better in previous years.

Company F is part of a group of food companies which has operations in Scotland and England. The company naturally cooperates and networks with other food companies in the same group. There is no evidence of collaboration in new product development, as each one of these company has its unique food range. The company, however, has regular contact and collaboration with its customers, particularly Waitrose and Marks & Spencer whose representatives participate in the validation of products being developed by the company.

There is no evidence of Company G's participation in any cooperative or networking initiative with other food companies, its customers or suppliers. The Company G entrepreneur however, did say that she thought Scottish Enterprise was very helpful and had been 'good' to the company.

Cooperation and networking: Cross-case analysis

Table 6.1 shows the evidence on cooperation and networking by the case study companies. All seven investigated enterprises render proof of some kind of cooperation and networking with external bodies. Only four enterprises, however, use cooperation and networking for new product development, with only one company cooperating for new product development with other food companies.

Table 6.1 Cooperation and networking by the case study companies

Company	Cooperation	With	For
A	Yes	Other food companies, Scottish Enterprise	Marketing
B	Yes	Other food companies, suppliers, customers	New product development
		Scottish Enterprise	Training, design develop-ment, marketing, cash flow
C	Yes	supplier	New product development
D	Yes	Other food companies	Acquisition of equipment
		Scottish Enterprise	Feasibility studies
E	Yes	Scottish Enterprise	New product development
F	Yes	Other companies in the same group	General cooperation
		Customers	New product development
G	Yes	Scottish Enterprise	General help

Financial resources, human resources and managerial efficiency: Within-case analysis

Research analysing the inability of small firms to be consistently innovative indicates inadequate marketing and management skills as the main reason (Moore, 1995). This in turn is caused by problems in obtaining and grooming requisite managerial talent since these firms cannot afford the pay and prerequisites that the large firms usually provide (Grieve-Smith & Fleck, 1987 and Beaver & Prince, 2002). The managerial inefficacy thus springs from financial inadequacy, as typical small firms lack financial resources resulting in inadequate recruitment of human resources. This makes it difficult for them to innovate successfully. Innovative aspirations of SMEs thus are circumscribed by a vicious cycle, which has financial, managerial and human resources aspects. This also means the three independently identified determinants of innovation, namely, human resources, managerial efficiency and financial resources are intertwined in the case of small firms and are therefore analysed together here.

Company A has successfully created new products and taken them to the market without the use of large financial or managerial resources because the company has strong internal capability in understanding a route to successful innovation and reaching its innovation goals. The company is dependent on idea generation and implementation on a small well-knit team made up of the entrepreneur, his father and the technical manager. Innovation is not expensive in this organisation because the enterprise does not need to invest additional resources in hiring experts, as the entrepreneur and his team work on innovation concurrently with other tasks in the organisation. The marketing inability mentioned in the literature is overcome by the company through collaboration with other Scottish food companies to market collectively its products with the support from Scottish Enterprise. The company does not face any financial resource crunch because the money needed for innovation in this enterprise is not huge and is always within the company's means. It has no issues of human resources shortages bogging down the innovation process too, as it runs its innovation concurrently with its manufacturing, and depending on the needs of new product development, key people share roles and responsibilities.

Company B is part of a group of small companies owned by a family which donates most of the profit generated by the companies to charity, although it always makes available any money needed for reinvestment before allocating the rest to the charity. It is understood that the family's ability to serve the charities close to its heart depends on the size of profits earned by the companies under its ownership, which in turn depends on exploitation of all profitable investment opportunities. In fact, when the group owners bought Company B, they invested so generously in it that Company B's 5-year investment plan was completed in 1 year. As a result of its financial well-being, unlike other small companies, Company B has a product development team of four full-time employees. It is located in a small town. When asked if this location makes it difficult for the company to attract or retain employees, the executive answered, "No. Actually, we've found it quite beneficial." Company B thus faces no problems in raising enough money to finance its innovation, nor does it faces any problems attracting and retaining a managerial workforce to carry out innovation. As Company B has been a successful innovator in its line of products, the finance that needs to carry out its innovation activities is always made available to it.

Company C does not seem to lack any managerial talent. The four individuals that collectively own the company have previously occupied high managerial positions in a large bakery, and each one of them has significant managerial experience. These top managers carry out new product development, without major involvement of other staff. As new product ideas occur and are validated, financial plans are made for each. These plans are then stored away. When the company is negotiating new products to supply to its major customers, it apprises them of all of its product plans. If a customer shows willingness to put on shelf any one of the company's new products, it then implements the plan and develops the product. And so it tackles the problem of financial resources by not developing new products without assuring that its major customers, the superstores, are willing to place orders for them.

Company D is run by a husband and wife team who have complementary skills. The husband is very creative and keeps coming out with great new ideas. The wife, in contrast, is pragmatic and decides which of her husband's ideas is feasible. She is also able to execute the chosen ideas successfully. The company initially raised resources for market research but subsequently has been developing and marketing its own products due the entrepreneurs' evolved understanding of their market and their products. The company has also been able to raise resources for innovation because the entrepreneurs have reinvested all their earnings into the enterprise. The company has also done well financially, and its revenue has grown at 20% per annum against 5% growth in volume. Company D does not need extra managerial resources as the husband and wife team of entrepreneurs running this company have all the necessary skills to carry out innovation. The entrepreneurs' commitment to new product development extends to denying themselves any substantial salaries.

Company E does not appear to have any financial problems in developing or marketing its products. For a company employing only three people, yet having an annual turnover of 3.4 million, the business is well endowed with financial resources. It has been able to carry out its modest incremental innovation easily, without facing any managerial or financial problems. Given the low-key low-tech nature of its new product development, it does not need resources beyond its grasp. As it does not supply to superstores but mostly exports its goods, its margins are decent, and it has been able to fund its projects. The none-too-ambitious nature of its product development also means that the entrepreneur does not need to employ experts to guide its product development process. As the company has a policy of outsourcing all its activities, it is able to hire requisite services when need be.

Company F, too, does not face any managerial or financial constraints to its new product development efforts. There are two main reasons for this. The company is a part of a thriving group of small enterprises that supports each other financially, and the company on its own is quite profitable and growing. At the time of investigation, its annual turnover was £16 million. It subsequently invested in a state-of-the-art manufacturing facility, which again shows that there are no financial constraints affecting its activities. Because the company has a full-time product development executive and a product development department shows that innovation at Company F is not hampered by a paucity of functional experts.

Company G, founded and run by two budding entrepreneurs, is committed to popularise organic food. The company's new product development is run by these two individuals. The company also employs a nutrition expert, but the entrepreneurs themselves are very knowledgeable about organic food and health foods. The company thus has been able to develop successfully its new products without feeling any constraints in terms of lack of personnel. Because food sector innovation, being low-tech, does not need large financial resources, the company is able to raise them without any problems. Often at Company G, as many as six new products are being developed at the same time. The company at the time of this investigation had a staff of 40 carefully chosen people. The entrepreneur said that able to fit into the team was a critical element in bring new staff on board – although this was a rare event.

Financial resources, human resources and managerial efficiency: Cross-case analysis

These companies are able to engage in innovation and new product development without any significant financial restraint. There are no signs of a shortage of a competent managerial workforce. All these enterprises have been able to attract and retain requisite managerial talent. Another significant fact is that in most of these companies the entrepreneurs themselves are skilled, capable of performing on the innovation front and do not require much outside recruitment for the purpose. These organisations have also succeeded in developing their markets well without any major advertising or marketing effort.

Analysis of age

The work on influence of age of the enterprise on innovation was initiated by Schumpeter (1934). From his examination of the late-19th-century industrial structure in Europe, he observed that small firms using new technology are able to enter a competitive industry easily. He therefore theorised that the small new firms are major drivers of innovation and argued that successful new firms usher in new ideas, products and processes. Their appearance thus disrupts existing arrays of organisation, production and distribution and eliminates the quasi-rents, resulting from previous innovations. He refers to this dynamics, 'creative destruction'. In later literature, this has been labelled as a *Schumpeter Mark I* pattern of innovation (Fontana *et al.*, 2012).

This research, however, does not corroborate the Schumpeter theorem. The case study companies are not young nascent enterprises trying to enter an industry dominated by large companies, and they do not use innovation as an instrument to facilitate this.

There is also no evidence of these enterprises causing any creative destruction by eradicating the large food companies in Scotland. The case study companies are not 'young'. The youngest of them was in business for 11 years in 2008. The mean age of these enterprises is over 22 years. The belief that innovative companies are very young is thus not reflected in the age profile of these companies. It is also not so that the age of these companies are skewed on the side of low age companies. They are in fact equally distributed on both sides of the mean age, with half of the companies older than the mean age and other half younger than the mean age. There is thus no evidence to show that being young is an influence on these organisations' innovativeness.

The reason for this research not supporting the Schumpeterian hypothesis is, however, not difficult to understand. Schumpeter's conclusions are based on his observation of new technology start-ups that were active in high-technology industries. The companies investigated in this research, in contrast, are from the low-tech food sector, where the age obviously has no influence on the ability of enterprise to innovate successfully.

Analysis of size

As all companies investigated in this research were SMEs at the time of investigation, differences in the role of determinants of innovation between small and large companies are not discussed here.

Key concepts emerging from the case studies

Key concepts that emerge from the above analysis are presented in Table 6.2.

Table 6.2 Summary of key emerging concepts

From the analysis of *Process of Innovation*	In the food industry, new product development and new packaging development occur simultaneously.
	Food innovators constantly travel and eat new varieties of foods at varied locations to identify new product ideas.
	Innovative food companies sell most of their new products to very large retailers, such as superstores or up-market grocery chains.
	Innovative small food companies remain in regular contact with their main customers throughout the product development process.
	New product development towards more luxuriant and expensive versions suits well the high-variety low-volume operations of small food companies.
	New products that are variants of a company's existing products have better success potential than the products that are significantly different.
	In case study companies, the basic innovation process is informal and cross-functional.
	In the Scottish food industry, innovation is not focused on the development of healthy foods.
From the analysis of *Market Orientation*	Innovative small food companies: • exhibit an ability to explore and reach potential markets. • demonstrate a good fit between market needs and the firm's resources. • have a good understanding of customer needs and user circumstances. • use production methods that are amenable to quick changes in final products.[1]

(Continued)

Table 6.2 (Continued)

From the analysis of *Learning Processes*	A knack to spot opportunities for innovation and continuous learning is observed in innovative small food companies.
From the analysis of *Technology Policy*	There is an absence of formal R&D in innovative small food companies.
From the analysis of *Cooperation and Networks*	In innovative small food companies, cooperation and networking exists with customers, suppliers, other food companies and Scottish Enterprise.
From the analysis of Financial and *Human Resources and Managerial Efficiency*	Innovative small food companies: • are able to attract and retain requisite talent for new product development. • do not face significant financial constraints in new product development. • demonstrate the ability to develop markets without major advertising or marketing efforts. • are able to attract and retain requisite talent for new product development.
From the analysis of *Age of Enterprise*	In the Scottish food industry, innovation is independent of the age of enterprise.
From the analysis of *Innovative People*	Creative people with high innovative proclivity play crucial roles in new product development in case study companies

[1] Also from the analysis of process of innovation

Note

1 All names within quotes have been changed for confidentiality.

References

Angle, H L (1989) Psychology and organisational innovation, in Van De Ven, A H, Angle, H L and Pool, M S (Eds) *Research on the Management of Innovation,* New York: Harper & Row, 135–70

Beaver, Graham and Prince, Christopher (2002) Innovation, entrepreneurship and competitive advantage in the entrepreneurial venture, *Journal of Small Business and Enterprise Development,* 9(1):28–37

Cooper, R G (1984) New product strategies: What distinguishes the top performers?, *Journal of Product Innovation Management*, 1(2):151–64

Cooper, R G (1994) New products: The factors that drive success, *International Marketing Review*, 11(1):60–76

De Brentani, U (2001) Innovative versus incremental new business services: Different keys to achieving success, *Journal of Product Innovation Management*, 18(3):169–87

Edgett, S. and Parkinson, S. (1994) The development of new financial services: Identifying determinants of success and failure, *International Journal of Service Industry Management*, 5(4):24–38

European Commission (2004) *Innovation in Europe: Results for the EU, Iceland and Norway Data 1998–2001*, Luxembourg, Sweden: Commission of the European Communities

Fontana, Roberto, Nuvolari, Alessandro, Shimizu, Hiroshi and Vezzulli, Andrea (2012) Schumpeterian patterns of innovation and the sources of breakthrough inventions: Evidence from a data-set of R&D awards, *Journal of Evolutionary Economics*, 22(4):785–810

Grieve-Smith, A and Fleck, V (1987) Business strategies in small high technology companies, *Long Range Planning*, 20(2):61–8

Heydebreck, Peter (1997) Technological Interweavement: A means for new technology-based firms to achieve innovation success, in Jones-Evans, Dylan and Klofsten, Magnus (Eds) *Technology, Innovation and Enterprise: The European Experience*, London: Macmillan Press

Hughes, R (1980) *The Shock of the New Art and the Century of Change*, Revised Edition 1991, London: Thames and Hudson

Hurley, R F and Hult, G T M (1998) Innovation, market orientation and organisational learning: An integration and empirical examination, *Journal of Marketing*, 62(3):42–54

IFICF (2011) Background on Functional Foods, www.foodinsight.org

Lindman, Martti Tapio (2002) Open or closed strategy in developing new products? A case study of industrial NPD in SMEs, *European Journal of Innovation Management*, 5(4):224–36

Moore, B (1995) What Differentiates Innovative Small Firms?, *Innovation Initiative Paper No. 4*, Cambridge: ESRC Centre for Business Research, University of Cambridge

Morgan, R E, Katsikeas, C S and Appiah-Adu, K (1998) Market orientation and organisational learning capabilities, *Journal of Marketing Management*, 4(4):353–81

Schumpeter, Joseph A (1934) *The Theory of Economic Development*, Cambridge, MA: Harvard University Press

Scottish Government (2007) *The Community Innovation Survey 4: Profiling Scotland's Innovation Performance*, Edinburgh: Scottish Government

Soderquist, Klas, Chanaron, J J and Motwani, Jaideep (1997) Managing innovation in French small and medium sized enterprises: an empirical study, *Benchmarking for Quality Management & Technology*, 4(4):259–72

Stata, R (1989) Organisational learning – the key to management innovation, *Sloan Management Review*, 30(3):63–74

Storey, C and Easingwood, C J (1996) Determinants of new product performance: A study in the financial services sector, *International Journal of Service Industry Management*, 7(1):32–55

7 New product development in Scotland

A survey

Introduction

To triangulate the case study results, a survey of Scottish companies that have successfully developed new products was carried out. Before embarking on the survey, the case study results were carefully reconsidered and edited. A set of emergent propositions based on the findings evident in most of the case study companies was then crystallised, and a survey questionnaire to test these propositions was developed. For ease of use for respondents and quick and error-free transfer of data to statistical computer programmes, an 'online' rather than a 'postal' survey was chosen. The online survey questionnaire on 'SurveyMonkey' was pretested by Mr Robin Pollok, a director of Food Initiative Limited, and modified further by incorporating his feedback. The web addresses of Scottish companies in the selected sectors were gleaned from the directory of Scottish businesses on the Scottish Enterprise website. The companies that made a claim of development of new products on their websites were contacted via emails sent to the person named 'contact person' on the Scottish Enterprise website. The emails included a cover letter and a link to the online survey.

Of 276 companies that could be contacted, 88 responded to the survey, of which 85 have returned complete and usable responses. In the data analysis on *SPSS.18* and *Minitab.15*, all 85 responses are first processed to test the emergent propositions. To gain further insights, the data is then divided into the following subgroups for segregated testing of survey propositions.

1 High-tech and low-tech companies
2 Food and drinks companies and non-food and drinks companies
3 New companies[1] and old companies[2]
4 Small companies[3] and larger companies.[4]

The exercise highlights interesting differences within these groups, which are discussed and summarised at the end of this chapter.

Survey methodology

The questionnaire development

To develop the survey questionnaire, the propositions to be tested are crystallised in four steps. First, the case study analysis of indicators of three main determinants of innovation, *Market Orientation, Learning Processes* and *Technology Policy* are considered. The indicators evident in five or more enterprises are considered strong enough for inclusion. However, from amongst these indicators, 'knack to spot opportunities for innovation' and 'successful development of new products' are excluded despite high incidence, as their presence is inevitable in the targeted companies. From the analysis of *Cooperation and Networking*, four principal networking partners reported by the case study companies, namely, customers, suppliers, competitors and Scottish Enterprise, are included in the survey. From the analysis of *Financial Resources, Human Resources* and *Managerial Efficiency,* three key propositions emerge. These are (1) *innovative food companies are able to engage in innovation and new product development without any significant financial constraints,* (2) *they do not face a shortage of competent people to develop new products* and (3) *they demonstrate an ability to develop markets without any major advertising or marketing effort.* From the analysis of '*Process of Innovation*', the following findings are considered for inclusion in the survey questionnaire.

1   In the food industry, new product development and new packaging development occur simultaneously.
2   Innovative food companies sell most of their new products to very large retailers, such as superstores or up-market grocery chains.
3   Innovative food companies remain in regular contact with their main customers throughout the product development process.
4   New product development towards more luxuriant and expensive versions suits well the high-variety-low-volume operations of small food companies.
5   New products that are variants of a company's existing products have better success potential than the products that are significantly different.
6   In the food industry, the basic innovation process is informal and cross-functional.
7   In the Scottish food industry, innovation is not focused on the development of healthy foods.

Following is a list of the propositions that emerge from the previous exercise and the associated questions that are designed to test them.

Finding from the case studies:

New products that are variants of a company's existing products have better success potential than the products that are significantly different.

Question

Successful new products developed by us are very different from our existing products.

   (Survey question inversely worded, agreement refutes and disagreement confirms the finding)

Finding from the case studies:

New product development towards more luxuriant and expensive versions offer better value for money spent on innovation.

Question

Development of 'premium' products has provided my company better returns on money spent than development of 'low-cost' products.

Finding from the case studies:

New product development towards more luxuriant and expensive versions suits well the high-variety-low-volume operations of small food companies.

Question

I would describe my company as a 'low-volume-high-variety' business rather than a 'high-volume-low-variety' business.

   (The first part of this finding is tested by the preceding question)

Finding from the case studies:

Innovative companies use production methods that are amenable to quick changes in final products.

Question

Our flexible production methods allow us to alter and modify our products quickly.

Finding from the case studies:

Absence of formal R&D in innovative Scottish food companies

Question

There is no formal R&D department in our company.

Finding from the case studies:

Innovative food companies remain in regular contact with their main customers throughout the product development process.

Question

We remain in regular contact with our main customers during the development of new products.

Finding from the case studies:

Innovative food companies sell most of their new products to very large retailers, such as superstores or up-market grocery chains.

Question

We sell most of our new products to large retailers.

Finding from the case studies:

Creative people with high innovative proclivity play crucial roles in new product development in the food industry.

Question

The product development team in my company is made up of 'creative' people.

Finding from the case studies:

In the Scottish food industry, innovation is not focused on development of healthy foods.
    (No question asked to confirm this, as it is not applicable to nonfood companies.)

Finding from the case studies:

Innovative food companies exhibit an ability to explore and reach potential markets.

Question

Our success in new product development is due to our ability to identify and reach potential customers.

Finding from the case studies:

Innovative food companies exhibit a good fit between market needs and firm's resources.

Question

There is a good fit between what the market needs and what we can provide.

Finding from the case studies:

Continuous learning is observed in innovative food companies.

Question

We have been learning continuously from our efforts to develop new products.

Finding from the case studies:

Innovative food companies have a good understanding of customer needs and user circumstances.

Question

We understand the needs and circumstances of our customers very well.

Finding from the case studies:

Innovative food companies do not face significant financial constraints in new product development.

Question

We face financial constraints in our efforts to develop new products.
   (Survey question inversely worded, agreement refutes and disagreement confirms the finding)

Finding from the case studies:

In the food industry, new product development and new packaging development occur simultaneously.

(No questions are asked on this, as it is considered too specific to food companies.)

Finding from the case studies:

In the food industry, the basic innovation process is informal and cross-functional.

Two questions are used to confirm this.

1   *I would describe the innovation process in my company as informal.*
2   *People in my company working on new product development also perform other roles within the organisation.*

Finding from the case studies:

Innovative food companies are able to attract and retain requisite talent for new product development.

Question

We are able to recruit and retain the competent people needed for new product development.

Finding from the case studies:

Innovative food companies demonstrate an ability to develop markets without any major advertising or marketing effort.

Question

We are able to market our new products without any major advertising or marketing effort.

Finding from the case studies:

In innovative food companies cooperation and networking exists with customers, suppliers, competitors and Scottish Enterprise.

Question

For innovation we depend on close cooperation with . . . (Choose all those that apply to you).
   1. Our customers 2. Our suppliers 3. Our competitors 4. Scottish Enterprise 5. Others (please specify)

Finding from the case studies:

In the Scottish food industry, innovation is independent of the age of the enterprise.
   (This finding is attempted to be verified by including a question on the age cohort of the respondent companies.)

The survey process

Because the thrust of this research is on new product development, Scottish companies that have developed new products are identified and surveyed. As mentioned previously, to identify such companies, the directories of companies in various industry segments available on the Scottish Enterprise website were explored. It was observed that the Scottish Enterprise website classified Scottish businesses in the following segments:

1 Energy
2 Textiles
3 Life sciences
4 Digital markets
5 Aerospace, defence & marine
6 Tourism
7 Chemical sciences
8 Construction
9 Food and drinks
10 Financial services
11 Enabling technologies
12 Forest industries.

As surveys of this kind often do not generate a very high response rate, to have adequate responses for a meaningful analysis and generalisation of findings, tentatively about 350 companies were aimed to be identified. Mullen *et al.* (2009) advise a harmonious sample selection to 'strengthen internal validity'. As the original case studies are on the 'low tech' food industry, to triangulate the case study findings it was considered appropriate to look at companies in low-tech sectors of the Scottish economy. For this reason, the directories of *food and drinks, textiles* and *forest industry* companies were first explored. However, due to the absence of a directory of *forest industry* companies on the Scottish Enterprise website, only *food and drinks* and *textiles* companies were available for consideration. After browsing web pages of listed *food and drinks* and *textiles* companies that have their own websites, the companies that explicitly stated development of new products on their website were identified. However, this exercise led to the identification of less than 350 companies that had developed new products. This made it necessary to look for prospective respondents in other sectors. Of the remaining sectors listed on the Scottish Enterprise website, *tourism* and *financial services* were not considered because services are not the focus of this work, *aerospace* and *energy* were left out because they are dominated by very large companies not comparable to the case study companies and the *construction industry* was not targeted as preliminary exploration did not show evidence on development of new products by companies in this sector. Of the remaining industries, *life sciences* and *chemical science* were first explored, and companies in these two sectors, which made a claim of development of new products, were identified and emailed the survey questionnaire. When these were added to the already approached companies from *food and drinks* and *textiles* sectors, the number of contacted companies reached 348[5].

Unfortunately, due to the listing of emails of 'contact persons' on the Scottish Enterprise website not being up to date, a significant number of emails came back as 'undeliverable', and the number of companies which were effectively contacted was reduced to 276. The contacted Scottish companies, however, responded to the survey in good numbers, and the survey received 85 completed and useable responses, providing a response rate of 31%. Apart from a good response rate, the survey also has a very high completion rate. Out of total 1,955 expected answers from all respondents put together, only 21 (1%) in all are not provided.

The survey data

Self-selection bias

It is a possibility that the companies that respond to the survey may be different from those that do not, and so the data may have a self-selection bias. If this is so, the generalisation value of results is diminished. The standard procedure for checking for self-selection bias is to compare late responses to early responses using late response as a proxy for no response. Mullen *et al.* (2009:302) suggest, "Statistically nonsignificant differences on a number of descriptive variables (between early respondents and late respondents) indicate a lack of bias resulting from self-selection."

Table 7.1 Tests of normality

	Kolmogorov-Smirnov[a]			Shapiro-Wilk		
	Statistic	df	Sig.	Statistic	df	Sig.
Creative NPD team	.307	81	.000	.710	81	.000
Premiumisation, more lucrative	.295	81	.000	.807	81	.000
New products, very different	.163	81	.000	.927	81	.000
Low-volume high-variety business	.240	81	.000	.834	81	.000
Flexible production methods	.323	81	.000	.739	81	.000
No formal R&D	.274	81	.000	.788	81	.000
Regular customer contact	.294	81	.000	.758	81	.000
Large retailers, main customers	.270	81	.000	.823	81	.000
Informal innovation	.323	81	.000	.783	81	.000
Cross-functional innovation	.336	81	.000	.643	81	.000
Ability to explore markets	.244	81	.000	.870	81	.000
Good fit with market needs	.328	81	.000	.739	81	.000
Continuous learning	.286	81	.000	.679	81	.000
Financial constraints in NPD	.278	81	.000	.751	81	.000
Understanding of customer needs	.314	81	.000	.764	81	.000
Attracts and retains talent	.217	81	.000	.906	81	.000
No major marketing effort	.218	81	.000	.903	81	.000

[a]Lilliefors Significance Correction

Independent samples *t*-tests between early response and late response for equality of means and equality of variances are generally deployed for this purpose. However, independent samples *t*-tests assumes a normal distribution of responses (Dorofeev & Grant, 2006). The results for test of normality of distribution show that none of the responses to survey propositions is normal as shown in Table 7.1.

When the data is not normally distributed, nonparametric tests are recommended for data analysis (Gibbons, 1976; Moore *et al.*, 2003). As shown in Table 7.2, the nonparametric tests for comparison of median between 10 early response companies and 10 late response companies show that at a 95% confidence level there are no statistically significant differences in the median for any one of the 17 propositions between early and late responses. This implies that the data has no self-selection bias.

Table 7.2 Nonparametric tests between early response and late response

	Mann-Whitney U	Wilcoxon W	Z	Asymp. Sig. (2-tailed)	Exact Sig. [2*(1-tailed Sig.)]
Creative NPD team	49	104	−.081	.935	.971
Premiumisation, more lucrative	30.5	85.5	−1.569	.117	.143
New products, very different	43	98	−.539	.590	.631
Low-volume-high-variety business	48.5	103.5	−.117	.907	.912
Flexible production methods	45	100	−.418	.676	.739
No formal R&D	45	100	−.398	.691	.739
Regular customer contact	45.5	100.5	−.363	.717	.739
Large retailers, main customers	45	100	−.393	.694	.739
Informal innovation	45	100	−.390	.696	.739
Cross-functional innovation	50	105	.000	1.000	1.000
Ability to explore markets	49.5	104.5	−.039	.969	.971
Good fit with market needs	46	101	−.340	.734	.796
Continuous learning	38.5	93.5	−1.009	.313	.393
Financial constraints in NPD	46.5	101.5	−.278	.781	.796
Understanding of customer needs	30.5	85.5	−1.603	.109	.143
Attracts and retains talent	47.5	102.5	−.198	.843	.853
No major marketing effort	42	97	−.631	.528	.579

Survey findings

Analysis of general information

Segment-distribution of survey companies

The survey questionnaire listed the industry segments within which the responding companies were asked to identify themselves. If none of the segments accurately described their industry sector, they were asked to tick on 'others' and then provide a brief description. The industry segments, selected from the Scottish Business Statistics (2010) and mentioned in the survey questionnaire are as follows:

 1 Manufacture of food products and beverages
 2 Manufacture of tobacco products
 3 Manufacture of textiles
 4 Manufacture of wearing apparel; dressing and dyeing of fur
 5 Manufacture of leather and leather products
 6 Manufacture of wood and wood products
 7 Manufacture of pulp, paper and paper products
 8 Publishing, printing and reproduction of recorded media company
 9 Manufacture of rubber and plastic products
10 Manufacture of other nonmetallic mineral products
11 Manufacture of basic metals
12 Manufacture of fabricated metal products, except machinery and equipment
13 Manufacture of electrical machinery and apparatus not elsewhere classified
14 Manufacture of office machinery and computers
15 Manufacture of radio, television and communication equipment and apparatus
16 Manufacture of medical, precision and optical instruments, watches and clocks
17 Manufacture of motor vehicles, trailers and semi-trailers
18 Manufacture of other transport equipment
19 Manufacture of furniture manufacturing not elsewhere classified
20 Recycling company and
21 Other (please specify)

The distribution of respondent companies within different industry segments is shown in Figure 7.1. As food and drinks companies constituted the largest number of contacted businesses, the number of respondents from this sector constitutes the largest group. Of the remaining companies, a very large number (27) identified themselves as 'others'. However, a closer examination of how they have described themselves allowed many of them to be placed in one or the other of the listed categories, leaving only 5 in the 'others' category. Textile sector companies are divided into two segments *wearing apparel and dressing* and *textile*, depending on how they have placed themselves, or in case they have placed themselves in 'others' how they have described themselves. Companies in 'life science' sector are placed in *medical and precision instruments and products* or *IT software*, again depending on how they have placed themselves or how they have described themselves. Two of the companies however, have not given any response to the first part of the questionnaire that included questions on industry sector, age and employment. These are shown in Figure 7.1 as 'unknown'.

Age distribution of survey companies

Figure 7.2 depicts the age distribution of survey companies and shows that the survey companies are fairly well distributed across various age cohorts.

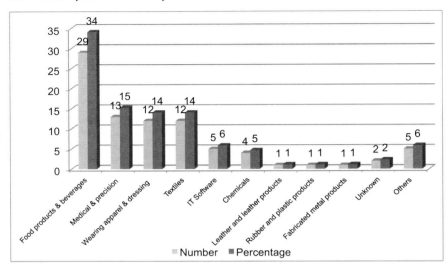

Figure 7.1 Segment distribution of survey companies

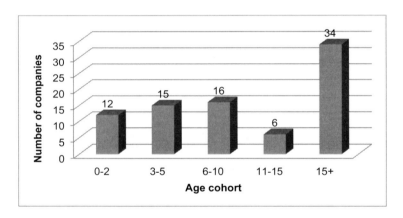

Figure 7.2 Age distribution of survey companies

The largest number of respondents, however, is in the age group of 15+ years. It appears that the Schumpeterian Mark I hypothesis (Fontana *et al.*, 2012) that nascent enterprises lead the thrust for innovation is not observed in Scotland. This issue is further investigated later in this chapter.

Time to innovate

The survey companies were asked two questions: how long they have been in business and how long they have been developing new products. Most of

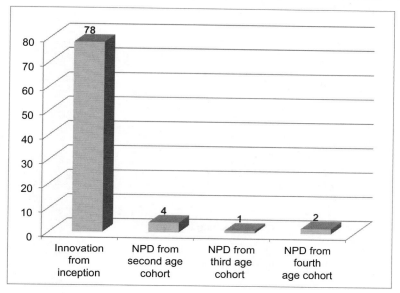

Figure 7.3 Commencement of new product development

them (89%) have ticked in the same age cohort for both of these questions. This means that these companies have been developing new products almost from inception. This is shown in the Figure 7.3.

Size distribution of survey companies

Although the sample companies are not very young, they indeed are predominantly small, as is obvious from Figure 7.4. Eighty-five percent of respondent companies have fewer than 50 employees, and 95% are SMEs. From this, it may appear that smaller companies are overrepresented in this sample. This, however, is not the case, as shown in Figure 7.5 that compares Scottish companies with the survey companies in different size groups.

62% of Scottish companies are in the lowest employment band of 1 to 4 employees, whereas there are only 33% survey companies in this band. As we move towards higher employment bands, we observe proportionately more survey companies in comparison to companies in Scotland in general. This suggests that very small Scottish companies have not been able to create new products successfully, whereas amongst the relatively larger companies, successful product innovators are in greater proportions. This issue is further investigated through a one-sample *t*-test and its implications discussed later in this chapter.

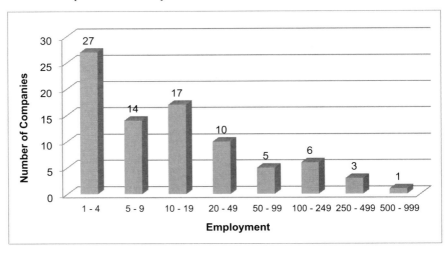

Figure 7.4 Size distribution of survey companies

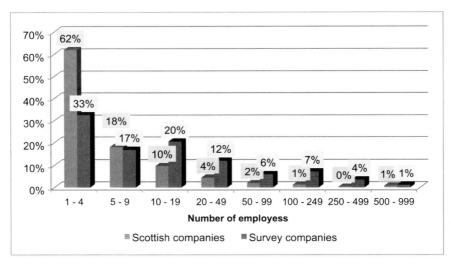

Figure 7.5 Size distribution of companies: Survey versus Scotland

Source for Scottish companies: Scottish Government, 2012

Analysis of information on innovation

The preliminary survey results for new product development by the responding companies are presented in Table 7.3. The first column shows the relevant survey question. The next column, titled '% Agree', depicts total percentage of companies that responded either as strongly agree, agree or mildly agree

Table 7.3 The preliminary survey results

Proposition	% Agree	% Disagree	% Neutral
We have been learning continuously from our efforts to develop new products.	98.8	1.2	0
People in my company working on new product development also perform other roles within the organisation (Cross-functional innovation).	90.6	7.1	2.4
The product development team in my company is made up of 'creative' people.	90.6	7.1	2.4
Our flexible production methods allow us to alter and modify our products quickly.	90.6	5.9	3.5
We understand the needs and circumstances of our customers very well.	91.8	2.4	4.7
We remain in regular contact with our main customers during the development of new products.	89.4	4.7	5.9
There is a good fit between what the market needs and what we can provide.	90.6	3.5	4.7
Development of 'premium' products has provided my company better returns on money spent than development of 'low-cost' products.	81.2	5.9	12.9
I would describe my company as a 'low-volume-high-variety' business rather than a 'high-volume-low-variety' business.	74.1	11.8	12.9
I would describe the innovation process in my company as informal.	76.5	20	2.4
There is no formal R&D department in my company.	67.1	27.1	4.7
Our success in new product development is due to our ability to explore and reach potential markets.	75.3	9.4	14.1
We are able to develop markets for our new products without any major advertising or marketing effort.	69.4	21.2	9.4
We are able to recruit and retain the competent people needed for new product development.	55.3	15.3	28.2
We face financial constraints in our efforts to develop new products.	80	14.1	4.7
We sell most of our new products to large retailers.	17.6	70.6	8.2
Successful new products developed by us are very different from our existing products.	47.1	24.7	28.2

to the question. The next column titled '% Disagree' shows total percentage of those that responded either as strongly disagree, disagree or mildly disagree to the question whereas percentage of companies that responded neither agree nor disagree are shown as 'Neutral' in the last column.

For a more precise presentation of the levels of agreements and disagreements to the survey questions, the responses are given varying weights to capture the strength of agreement versus the strength of disagreement. For this purpose the range of responses are coded in the following manner in Table 7.4.

In Table 7.5, the sum of all positive responses is depicted as 'acceptance index' and the sum of all negative responses is shown as 'rejection index'. The zero value responses are ignored and the indices are normalised to account for missing values.

Table 7.4 Response codes

Strongly agree	Agree	Mildly agree	Neither agree nor disagree	Mildly disagree	Disagree	Strongly disagree
3	2	1	0	−1	−2	−3

Table 7.5 Survey propositions: Acceptance and rejection indices

Proposition	Acceptance Index	Rejection Index
We have been learning continuously from our efforts to develop new products.	204	2
People in my company working on new product development also perform other roles within the organisation (cross-functional innovation).	194	11
The product development team in my company is made up of 'creative' people.	189	8
Our flexible production methods allow us to alter and modify our products quickly.	180	7
We understand the needs and circumstances of our customers very well.	180	3
We remain in regular contact with our main customers during the development of new products.	179	6
There is a good fit between what the market needs and what we can provide.	174	6
Development of 'premium' products has provided my company better returns on money spent than development of 'low-cost' products.	163	7

(Continued)

Table 7.5 (Continued)

Proposition	Acceptance Index	Rejection Index
I would describe my company as a 'low-volume-high-variety' business rather than a 'high-volume-low-variety' business.	147	19
I would describe the innovation process in my company as informal.	143	31
There is no formal R&D department in my company.	142	50
Our success in new product development is due to our ability to explore and reach potential markets.	133	14
We are able to develop markets for our new products without any major advertising or marketing effort.	108	31
We are able to recruit and retain the competent people needed for new product development.	93	21
We face financial constraints in our efforts to develop new products.	169	24
We sell most of our new products to large retailers.	25	142
Successful new products developed by us are very different from our existing products.	70	38

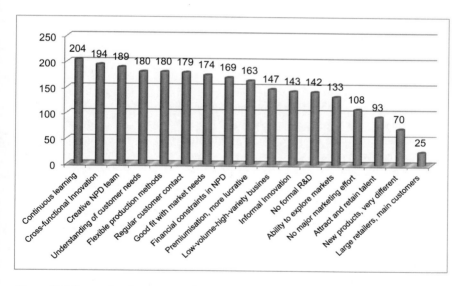

Figure 7.6 Strength of agreement for survey propositions

Figure 7.6 lists the survey propositions ranked in order of their normalised acceptance indices.

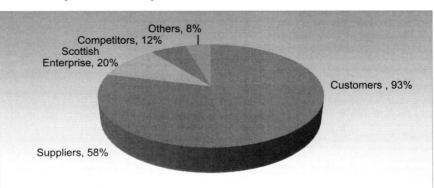

Figure 7.7 Partners in innovation

Networking for innovation

The survey reveals that for new product development, the responding companies network principally with their customers and suppliers. Very few (only 20%) network with Scottish Enterprise for the purpose. One interesting finding not obvious in Figure 7.7 is that amongst the 'other' networking partners mentioned by the survey companies, only two companies have specified academic institutions as 'others'. This shows that Scottish universities' involvement with Scottish companies in new product development is negligible.

Testing of hypotheses

For a more rigorous verification of survey results, further tests are conducted using the statistical programmes *SPSS.16* and *Minitab.15*. For this purpose, each statement listed on page 2 of the questionnaire is taken as a hypothesis and the response data is used to test it. As the responses range from 'strongly agree' to 'strongly disagree' on a 7-point scale, in order to code them for statistical data analysis they are transformed, as mentioned earlier, in the following manner:

Table 7.6 Response codes

Strongly agree	Agree	Mildly agree	Neither agree nor disagree	Mildly disagree	Disagree	Strongly disagree
3	2	1	0	−1	−2	−3

As the data generated by this survey, as shown earlier, is not normally distributed, for the testing of hypotheses, the Wilcoxon Signed Rank Test, a widely used nonparametric test is, conducted on the survey data, and the results are displayed in Table 7.7.

The test results show that for 16 propositions, with $p > .05$ the null hypotheses ($\mu = 0$) is rejected and consequently the alternate hypothesis ($\mu > 0$) is accepted at a 95% significance level. One proposition that is not supported by the test is:

1   Innovative companies sell most of their new products to very large retailers.

This means that the above proposition coming from the case studies of seven food companies cannot be generalised in a wider Scottish context.

$H_0: \mu = 0; \quad H_1: \mu > 0$

Table 7.7 Wilcoxon Signed Rank Test: All companies, all propositions

	N	N*	N for Test	Wilcoxon Statistic	P	Estimated Median
Creative NPD team	85	0	83	3413.0	0.00	2.50
Premiumisation, more lucrative	85	0	74	2694.5	0.00	2.00
New products, very different	85	0	61	1202.0	0.033	0.50
Low-volume-high-variety business	84	1	73	2423.5	0.00	1.50
Flexible production methods	85	0	82	3328.0	0.00	2.00
No formal R&D	84	1	80	2389.5	0.00	1.00
Regular customer contact	85	0	80	3159.5	0.00	2.00
Large retailers, main customers	82	3	75	342.0	1.00	−1.50
Informal innovation	84	1	82	2836.5	0.00	1.50
Cross-functional innovation	85	0	83	3351.5	0.00	2.50
Ability to explore markets	84	1	72	2392.5	0.00	1.50
Good fit with market needs	84	1	80	3136.5	0.00	2.00
Continuous learning	85	0	85	3630.0	0.00	2.50
Financial constraints in NPD	84	1	80	2893.5	0.00	2.00
Understanding of customer needs	84	1	80	3205.5	0.00	2.00
Attracts and retains talent	84	1	60	1521.0	0.00	1.00
No major marketing effort	85	0	77	2321.0	0.00	1.00

It is pertinent to note here that two survey questions are inversely worded. Their acceptance means the rejection of relevant case study findings and their rejection means the acceptance of relevant case study findings. These are:

2   Successful new products developed by us are very different from our existing products.
3   We face financial constraints in our efforts to develop new products.

In the test based on survey results, both the above propositions are accepted. It means that case study findings inherent in these propositions are not corroborated by the larger survey. It also means that out of 17 case study findings attempted to be verified by the Scotland-wide survey, three have not been confirmed. To see if these have support within the food and drinks companies in the sample, the Wilcoxon Signed Rank Test is rerun exclusively for the 29 food and drinks companies in the sample, and the results are shown in Table 7.8.

$$H_0: \mu = 0; \qquad H_1: \mu > 0$$

Table 7.8 Wilcoxon Signed Rank Test: Food and drinks companies

	N	Test	Statistic	P	Median
Creative NPD team	29	28	380.0	0.000	2.000
Premiumisation, more lucrative	29	28	377.5	0.000	2.000
New products, very different	**29**	**23**	**154.0**	**0.637**	**0.000**
Low-volume-high-variety business	29	24	288.0	0.000	2.000
Flexible production methods	29	29	426.5	0.000	2.500
No formal R&D	29	28	338.5	0.002	2.000
Regular customer contact	29	26	329.5	0.000	2.000
Large retailers, main customers	29	26	74.5	0.011	−1.000
Informal innovation	29	29	412.5	0.000	2.000
Cross-functional innovation	29	29	421.0	0.000	2.500
Ability to explore markets	29	26	318.0	0.000	1.500
Good fit with market needs	29	28	383.0	0.000	2.000
Continuous learning	29	29	426.0	0.000	2.500
Financial constraints in NPD	29	27	342.5	0.000	2.000
Understanding of customer needs	29	27	367.0	0.000	2.000
Attracts and retains talent	**29**	**17**	**90.0**	**0.538**	**0.000**
No major marketing effort	29	28	370.0	0.000	1.50

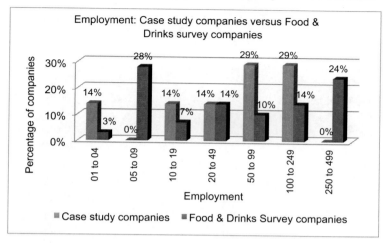

Figure 7.8 Employment: Case study companies versus survey companies

The exercise shows that the proposition '*Innovative companies sell most of their new products to very large retailers*' is not rejected by the food and drinks companies' survey data. Interestingly the test exclusively for food and drinks companies also show that the case study finding that new products developed by innovative companies are variants of their existing products is true in this case as well. However, the case study finding on *no financial constraints in NPD* and ability of innovative companies to *attract and retain requisite talent* is not supported by the test of response from food and drinks companies in the survey. A possible reason for this variance between 7 case study companies and 29 survey companies in the same food and drinks sector could be a difference in size distribution of the two groups as shown in the Figure 7.8.

Table 7.9 shows how the test results for food companies contrast with non-food and drinks companies.

For 53 non-food and drinks companies, the Wilcoxon Signed Rank Test does not support the same proposition rejected by the tests involving all 85 companies; however, the test in this case additionally rejects one additional proposition relating to new products being very different from the existing products.

Segregated data analysis

In order to understand if there are further significant differences in responses from specific groups of responding companies, a series of additional tests are carried out.

$$H_0: \mu = 0; \qquad H_1: \mu > 0$$

Table 7.9 Wilcoxon Signed Rank Test: Non-food and drinks companies

	N	N*	N for Test	Wilcoxon Statistic	P	Estimated Median
Creative NPD team	53	0	52	1372.0	0.000	2.50
Premiumisation, more lucrative	53	0	43	941.0	0.000	2.00
New products, very different	53	0	35	413.0	0.055	0.50
Low-volume-high-variety business	52	1	47	992.5	0.000	2.00
Flexible production methods	53	0	50	1241.5	0.000	2.00
No formal R&D	52	1	49	833.0	0.014	0.50
Regular customer contact	53	0	51	1317.0	0.000	2.50
Large retailers, main customers	50	3	46	72.5	1.000	−2.00
Informal innovation	52	1	50	977.0	0.001	1.50
Cross-functional innovation	53	0	51	1268.5	0.000	2.50
Ability to explore markets	52	1	43	854.5	0.000	1.50
Good fit with market needs	52	1	49	1200.0	0.000	2.00
Continuous learning	53	0	53	1431.0	0.000	2.50
Financial constraints in NPD	52	1	50	1137.0	0.000	2.50
Understanding of customer needs	52	1	50	1271.5	0.000	2.00
Attracts and retains talent	52	1	40	742.5	0.000	1.00
No major marketing effort	53	0	46	758.0	0.009	1.00

High-tech companies versus low-tech companies.

To undertake this exercise, *food products and beverages, wearing apparel and dressing, textiles, leather and leather products, rubber and plastic products* and *fabricated metal products* companies are coded as low-tech enterprises (Table 7.10) whereas *medical and precision instruments and products, IT software* and *chemicals* companies are coded as high tech (Table 7.11). The exact description provided by respondents in case of five companies listed as 'others' is used to decide on their place in one of these two categories. One company that did not reveal its industry segments and two companies listed as 'unknown' are excluded from this analysis.

$$H_0: \mu = 0; \qquad H_1: \mu > 0$$

Table 7.10 Wilcoxon Signed Rank Test: Low-tech companies

	N	N*	N for Test	Wilcoxon Statistic	P	Estimated Median
Creative NPD team	59	0	57	1611.0	0.000	2.500
Premiumisation, more lucrative	59	0	54	1434.5	0.000	2.000
New products, very different	59	0	45	638.0	0.088	0.500
Low-volume-high-variety business	58	1	51	1283.0	0.000	2.000
Flexible production methods	59	0	58	1693.0	0.000	2.500
No formal R&D	58	1	56	1357.0	0.000	2.000
Regular customer contact	59	0	54	1435.0	0.000	2.000
Large retailers, main customers	57	2	52	165.5	1.000	−1.500
Informal innovation	58	1	57	1521.0	0.000	2.000
Cross-functional innovation	59	0	58	1635.0	0.000	2.500
Ability to explore markets	59	0	50	1140.5	0.000	1.500
Good fit with market needs	58	1	54	1410.5	0.000	2.000
Continuous learning	59	0	59	1752.0	0.000	2.500
Financial constraints in NPD	58	1	56	1353.5	0.000	2.000
Understanding of customer needs	58	1	54	1462.0	0.000	2.000
Attract and retain talent	58	1	37	540.5	0.002	0.500
No major marketing effort	59	0	53	1253.0	0.000	1.500

The results show that in case of 59 low-tech enterprises the test rejects two propositions, the same that is rejected by the test involving all 85 companies and one more, namely, *new products, very different from the existing products*, whereas in case of 23 high-tech enterprise, beyond the one rejected by the test involving all 85 companies, the test rejects three other propositions, namely, *new products, very different from the existing products, no formal R&D, informal innovation* and *no major marketing effort*. As stated earlier the rejection of proposition *new products, very different from the existing products* actually means acceptance of finding of the case studies. For high-tech enterprises, rejection of propositions on 'no formal R&D', 'informal innovation' and 'no major marketing effort' is consistent with previous research on high-tech innovation.

New companies versus old companies

To see how more recently established companies compare with companies that are operating for longer period in their response to various survey

$H_0: \mu = 0;$ $H_1: \mu > 0$

Table 7.11 Wilcoxon Signed Rank Test: High-tech companies

	N	N*	N for Test	Wilcoxon Statistic	P	Estimated Median
Creative NPD team	23	0	23	272.0	0.000	2.50
Premiumisation, more lucrative	23	0	18	167.0	0.000	1.50
New products, very different	23	0	15	88.0	0.059	0.50
Low-volume-high-variety business	23	0	19	141.0	0.034	1.00
Flexible production methods	23	0	21	210.5	0.001	1.50
No formal R&D	23	0	22	113.0	0.675	0.00
Regular customer contact	23	0	23	274.0	0.000	2.50
Large retailers, main customers	22	1	20	33.0	0.997	−1.00
Informal innovation	23	0	22	174.0	0.064	0.50
Cross-functional innovation	23	0	22	252.0	0.000	2.50
Ability to explore markets	22	1	20	198.5	0.000	1.50
Good fit with market needs	23	0	23	276.0	0.000	2.50
Continuous learning	23	0	23	276.0	0.000	2.50
Financial constraints in NPD	23	0	21	231.0	0.000	3.00
Understanding of customer needs	23	0	23	276.0	0.000	2.50
Attracts and retains talent	23	0	20	194.0	0.000	1.50
No major marketing effort	23	0	22	146.5	0.263	0.50

questions, a Wilcoxon Signed Rank Test is run after segregating responses for 43 companies that are 10 or less years old and that of 40 companies that are more than 10 years old, and the results are displayed in Table 7.12 and Table 7.13, respectively. The results show that there is no difference in response from new companies aged 10 years or less and old companies aged 11 years or more, and each segregated sample rejects the same two propositions, one rejected by the test involving all 85 companies and one more, namely, *new products, very different from the existing products*. This confirms the case study finding that the age of enterprise has no role in influencing the innovative behaviour of Scottish companies. This is further corroborated by the independent sample *t*-test discussed later in this chapter.

$H_0: \mu = 0;$ $H_1: \mu > 0$

Table 7.12 Wilcoxon Signed Rank Test: Up to 10-year-old companies

	N	N*	N for Test	Wilcoxon Statistic	P	Estimated Median
Creative NPD team	43	0	43	923.5	0.000	2.50
Premiumisation, more lucrative	43	0	35	594.0	0.000	2.00
New products, very different	43	0	28	237.5	0.219	0.00
Low-volume-high-variety business	43	0	40	728.5	0.000	2.00
Flexible production methods	43	0	41	815.5	0.000	2.00
No formal R&D	43	0	41	658.5	0.002	1.00
Regular customer contact	43	0	39	745.0	0.000	2.00
Large retailers, main customers	42	1	37	47.0	1.000	−2.00
Informal innovation	43	0	42	768.0	0.000	2.00
Cross-functional innovation	43	0	42	899.0	0.000	2.50
Ability to explore markets	42	1	36	583.5	0.000	1.50
Good fit with market needs	43	0	40	787.0	0.000	2.50
Continuous learning	43	0	43	936.0	0.000	2.50
Financial constraints in NPD	43	0	40	787.0	0.000	2.50
Understanding of customer needs	43	0	41	846.0	0.000	2.00
Attracts and retains talent	43	0	30	363.5	0.004	1.00
No major marketing effort	43	0	41	651.0	0.002	1.00

Small companies versus larger companies

In order to see how small companies employing less than 50 people compare with larger companies that employ 50 or more people in their response to various survey questions, a Wilcoxon Signed Rank Test is run after segregating responses for 68 small companies and 15 large companies, and the results are displayed in Table 7.14 and Table 7.15.

The test involving the segregated sample of 68 small companies employing less than 50 people does not support the same proposition rejected by the tests involving all 85 companies; however, the test in this case additionally rejects one more proposition relating to new products being very different from the existing products. The test in case of 15 companies employing

$H_0: \mu = 0; \qquad H_1: \mu > 0$

Table 7.13 Wilcoxon Signed Rank Test: More than 10-year-old companies

	N	N*	N for Test	Wilcoxon Statistic	P	Estimated Median
Creative NPD team	40	0	38	724.5	0.000	2.00
Premiumisation, more lucrative	40	0	37	703.0	0.000	2.50
New products, very different	40	0	31	321.5	0.076	0.50
Low-volume-high-variety business	39	1	32	515.5	0.000	2.00
Flexible production methods	40	0	39	767.0	0.000	2.50
No formal R&D	39	1	38	579.0	0.001	2.00
Regular customer contact	40	0	39	773.0	0.000	2.50
Large retailers, main customers	38	2	36	149.5	0.998	−1.00
Informal innovation	39	1	38	677.5	0.000	2.00
Cross-functional innovation	40	0	39	728.0	0.000	2.50
Ability to explore markets	40	0	35	589.0	0.000	1.50
Good fit with market needs	39	1	38	722.0	0.000	2.00
Continuous learning	40	0	40	820.0	0.000	2.00
Financial constraints in NPD	39	1	38	652.0	0.000	2.00
Understanding of customer needs	39	1	37	700.5	0.000	2.00
Attracts and retains talent	39	1	27	327.0	0.000	1.00
No major marketing effort	40	0	35	528.0	0.000	1.00

50 or more people does not support the same proposition rejected by the tests involving all 85 companies; however, the test in this case additionally rejects one more proposition relating to no formal R&D. This has important implication. It means that smaller survey companies do not undertake formal R&D, and their innovation is incremental. In contrast, the larger companies invest in R&D, and their quest is for innovation that is more radical. Influence of size on innovative behaviour of Scottish companies is further corroborated by the independent sample *t*-test discussed later in this chapter.

$H_0: \mu = 0; \qquad H_1: \mu > 0$

Table 7.14 Wilcoxon Signed Rank Test: Companies employing less than 50

	N	N*	N for Test	Wilcoxon Statistic	P	Estimated Median
Creative NPD team	68	0	66	2179.5	0.000	2.500
Premiumisation, more lucrative	68	0	58	1699.0	0.000	2.000
New products, very different	68	0	48	719.5	0.090	0.500
Low-volume-high-variety business	67	1	62	1793.5	0.000	2.000
Flexible production methods	68	0	65	2088.5	0.000	2.000
No formal R&D	67	1	64	1659.0	0.000	1.500
Regular customer contact	68	0	64	2069.0	0.000	2.000
Large retailers, main customers	65	3	59	87.5	1.000	−2.000
Informal innovation	67	1	65	1836.5	0.000	2.000
Cross-functional innovation	68	0	67	2227.5	0.000	2.500
Ability to explore markets	67	1	57	1497.0	0.000	1.500
Good fit with market needs	67	1	63	1988.5	0.000	2.000
Continuous learning	68	0	68	2346.0	0.000	2.500
Financial constraints in NPD	67	1	65	1963.5	0.000	2.500
Understanding of customer needs	67	1	63	2012.5	0.000	2.000
Attracts and retains talent	67	1	44	779.0	0.000	1.000
No major marketing effort	68	0	63	1561.0	0.000	1.000

Influence of size: Further test

The graphical presentation of data shows that the sample companies are dominated by small companies. Those that employ less than 50 people are 85% of the responding companies. From this, it appears that more small companies are innovative in Scotland in comparison to their larger counterparts. As shown earlier, graphical comparison of size distribution of Scottish companies with that of survey companies suggests that the situation may be the other way around. This is confirmed by statistical testing. Calculations from data on size of employment in Scottish companies that employ 1 person or more show that mean employment in such Scottish companies is 17 persons (Scottish Business Statistics, 2012). The mean employment in survey companies is, however, 48.79. This means that survey companies are larger than Scottish companies are in general.

One sample *t*-test for the survey data shows that against a population mean size of 17 the mean size of survey companies is higher, and *this difference is*

$H_0: \mu = 0; \qquad H_1: \mu > 0$

Table 7.15 Wilcoxon Signed Rank Test: Companies employing 50 or more

	N	N for Test	Wilcoxon Statistic	P	Estimated Median
Creative NPD team	15	15	111.5	0.002	2.000
Premiumisation, more lucrative	15	15	107.5	0.004	2.000
New products, very different	15	12	62.5	0.036	1.000
Low-volume-high-variety business	15	9	40.0	0.022	1.000
Flexible production methods	15	15	120.0	0.000	2.000
No formal R&D	15	15	58.0	0.556	0.000
Regular customer contact	15	14	93.0	0.006	2.000
Large retailers, main customers	15	14	54.5	0.462	0.000
Informal innovation	15	15	104.0	0.007	1.500
Cross-functional innovation	15	14	91.0	0.009	2.000
Ability to explore markets	15	14	97.0	0.003	1.500
Good fit with market needs	15	15	106.5	0.004	2.000
Continuous learning	15	15	114.0	0.001	2.000
Financial constraints in NPD	15	13	78.0	0.013	1.500
Understanding of customer needs	15	15	113.5	0.001	2.000
Attracts and retains talent	15	14	100.0	0.002	1.500
No major marketing effort	15	13	75.5	0.020	1.000

Table 7.16 One-Sample *t*-test, employment

Employment				Test Value = 17		
	t	df	Sig. (2-tailed)	Mean Difference	95% Confidence Interval of the Difference	
					Lower	Upper
	5.358	84	.000	92.91176	58.4302	127.3934

statistical significant at a 95% confidence level. This should be interpreted to mean that ability of a business to innovate is influenced by its size, and larger Scottish companies are more likely to be innovative than their smaller counterparts[6].

Table 7.17 One-Sample *t*-test, age

Age					Test Value = 11.42	
	t	*df*	*Sig. (two-tailed)*	*Mean Difference*	95% Confidence Interval of the Difference	
					Lower	*Upper*
	.157	82	.876	.132	−1.54	1.81

Influence of age: Further test

As is seen in the graphical presentation of data, young companies in the sample are few and older companies are many, particularly companies that are over 15 years old. From this it appears that fewer younger companies are innovative than their older counterparts. Calculations from data on age distribution of Scottish companies (ONS, 2008), using 20 years as proxy age for the group '10 years or more', gives the mean age of Scottish companies in year 2008 as 11.42 years. The mean age in survey companies in comparison is 11.54. From this, in terms of age, the survey companies do not look very different from Scottish companies in general. One-sample *t*-test for the survey data also shows that the mean age of Scottish companies and the mean age of survey companies is *not significantly different* at 95% confidence level. This should be interpreted to mean that ability of a Scottish business to innovate is not influenced by its age[7].

Survey limitations

1 The conclusions drawn from this survey cannot be generalised to all sectors of the Scottish economy as the survey companies are drawn from a limited number of sectors.
2 The results for 15 larger companies may not be conclusive because of relatively small sample size.

Summary of survey results

A summary of results of triangulation survey for all responding companies as well as for each subgroup of responding companies in the segregated data analysis is given in Table 7.18.

Table 7.18 Summary of results of the triangulation survey

Survey propositions	All	Survey sub-groups							
		Low-Tech	High-Tech	Food & Drinks	Non-Food & Drinks	Age 0–10	Age >10	Emp <50	Emp 50+
		Number of companies							
	85	59	23	29	53	43	40	68	15
Creative NPD team	✓	✓	✓	✓	✓	✓	✓	✓	✓
Premiumisation, more lucrative	✓	✓	✓	✓	✓	✓	✓	✓	✓
New products, very different	✓	✗	✗	✗	✗	✗	✗	✗	✓
Low-volume-high-variety business	✓	✓	✓	✓	✓	✓	✓	✓	✓
Flexible production methods	✓	✓	✓	✓	✓	✓	✓	✓	✓
No formal R&D	✓	✓	✗	✓	✓	✓	✓	✓	✗
Regular customer contact	✓	✓	✓	✓	✓	✓	✓	✓	✓
Large retailers, main customers	✗	✗	✗	✗	✗	✗	✗	✗	✗
Informal innovation	✓	✓	✗	✓	✓	✓	✓	✓	✓
Ability to explore markets	✓	✓	✓	✓	✓	✓	✓	✓	✓
Cross-functional innovation	✓	✓	✓	✓	✓	✓	✓	✓	✓
Good fit with market needs	✓	✓	✓	✓	✓	✓	✓	✓	✓
Continuous learning	✓	✓	✓	✓	✓	✓	✓	✓	✓
Financial constraints in NPD	✓	✓	✓	✓	✓	✓	✓	✓	✓
Understanding of customer needs	✓	✓	✓	✓	✓	✓	✓	✓	✓
Able to attract and retain talent	✓	✓	✓	✗	✓	✓	✓	✓	✓
No major marketing effort	✓	✓	✗	✓	✓	✓	✓	✓	✓

✓Proposition supported
✗Proposition refuted

Notes

1 Age 0–10 year
2 Age >10 years
3 Employment <50
4 Employment 50 or more
5 Companies on the Scottish Enterprise directories are loosely classified, and in each segment that was explored, many companies were discovered that did not logically belong to that sector. The companies were nonetheless chosen if evidence of development of new products was found. This explains why some of the responding companies are from sectors other than *Food and Drinks, Textiles, Life Sciences* and *Chemicals.*
6 This inference, however, has one limitation. Exact mean employment in Scottish companies as well as that in survey companies is not known.
7 This inference, however, has one limitation. Exact mean age of Scottish companies as well as that of survey companies is not known.

References

Dorofeev, S and Grant, P (2006) *Statistics for Real Life Surveys*, Cambridge: Cambridge University Press

Fontana, Roberto, Nuvolari, Alessandro, Shimizu, Hiroshi and Vezzulli, Andrea (2012) Schumpeterian patterns of innovation and the sources of breakthrough inventions: Evidence from a data-set of R&D awards, *Journal of Evolutionary Economics,* 22(4):785–810

Gibbons, Jean Dickinson (1976) *Nonparametric Methods for Quantitative Analysis*, New York: Holt, Rinehart and Winston

Moore, D S, McCabe G P, Duckworth W M & Sclove S L (2003) The practice of business statistics, New York, NY: W H Freeman

Mullen, Michael R, Budeva, Desislava G and Doney Patricia M (2009) Research methods in the leading small business–entrepreneurship journals: A critical review with recommendations for future research, *Journal of Small Business Management,* 47(3):287–307

ONS (2008) UK Business: Activity, Size and Locations, London: Office of National Statistics

Scottish Government (2012) Scottish Business Statistics, Edinburgh: Scottish Government

8   Conclusions and implications

Background

This research set out to investigate the process of innovation and new product development in the Scottish food SMEs. As no previous work exists in this area, exploratory case studies of seven small food companies were undertaken. The case studies revealed several key drivers of innovation in small food companies and distilled a distinct underlying process common to these enterprises and many of its little-known components. The case study findings were then triangulated through a larger survey of Scottish companies in food as well as nonfood sectors that have successfully developed new products. The survey confirmed most case study findings. However, as it involved companies in non-food & drinks sectors, larger companies as well as high-tech enterprises all different in various ways from the case study companies, a range of insights on innovation-process variation emanating from size, sector and technology-orientation also emerged.

Conceptual underpinnings of analysis: Definition of innovation

As articulated earlier, studies of innovation often result in very diverse and sometimes conflicting conclusions. This is attributed partly to lack of universally accepted definition of innovation (Le Bars *et al.*, 1998 and Grunert *et al.*, 1997) and partly to the fact that a wide heterogeneity of sources and outcomes makes innovation difficult to identify and analyse (Dosi, 1988). In an attempt to understand the reason behind the persistence of such incoherent notions of innovation amongst scholars, and to see if many known articulations of the innovation process can be logically juxtaposed in the same theoretical space, a set of selection of definitions of innovation were examined. The exercise led to the realisation that though the definitional writing on innovation includes several aspects of a large span of overlapping actions and outcomes, incorporating five definitive segments,[1] a particular definition might include only a certain few. Definitions dealing with uncommon segments thus appear to describe innovation differently. If we chart all elements of these five segments successively, we could visualise the full extent of an 'innovation span' within which all notions and definitions of innovation can be accommodated. The proposed innovation span affords a way out of an avoidable academic debate and advances our understanding of innovation. It also helps put any work on innovation in a proper context by positioning it within the span.

The usefulness of the notion of 'innovation span' becomes immediately obvious when we try to position the current research within it, as is shown in Figure 8.1.

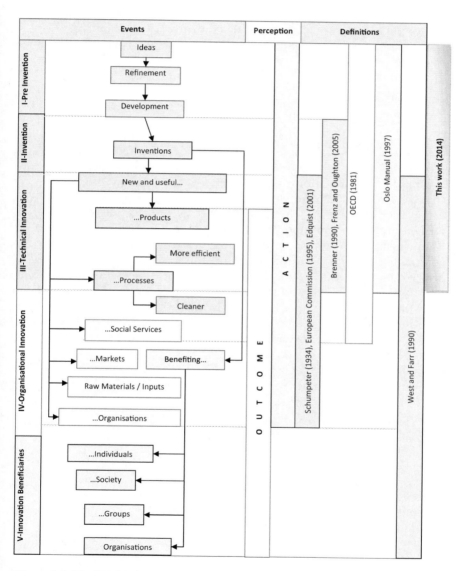

Figure 8.1 The innovation span revisited

Because this work explores the refinement and development of ideas into new and useful products and processes in the Scottish companies, it relates to Segments I, II and III of the innovation span. It is thus evident that the process of innovation in the Scottish food SMEs investigated here falls within the view of innovation articulated by OECD (1981), though, because of an obvious absence of social services in the companies investigated here, it is marginally different. On the other hand, though, this work analyses innovation on the same lines as suggested in the Oslo Manual (OECD, 1997) as well by Brenner (1990) and Frenz & Oughton (2005); by analysing the preinvention segment too, not considered by them, it goes beyond.

Its relative position vis-à-vis, definitions by West & Farr (1990), Schumpeter (1934), European Commission (1995) and Edquist (2001) can be similarly marked.

Taxonomy of innovation

During the course of this investigation, it was observed that innovation in the case study companies is geared largely towards technical innovation, and there is seemingly limited evidence of organisational innovation. Although organisational innovations, in the form of alterations in an organisation's structural and administrative procedures, are less evident here, there is, however, evidence of a whole gamut of activities that should be considered as organisational innovation exhibited by the case study companies. These include innovations in logistics, supply chain management and subcontracting. One interesting example of this is Company E, which found insurmountable obstacles in exporting haggis and other Scottish food products to the USA because of the restrictions imposed by the American Food and Drugs Administration. This company circumvented the problem by getting these products manufactured in Canada, as Canadian produce is not subject to such stringent conditions as the European food products are for import into the USA.

Similarly, many of these companies exhibited great ingenuity and deployed innovative methods to get round the problem of transporting small quantities of food to a very widespread market without compromising on the economies of scale.

In terms of product versus process innovation, the innovation in the case study companies is predominantly product focused. One reason for this is that relatively smaller case study companies, using two-stage idea validation serve a niche market and do not need any changes in existing manufacturing to produce new products. These companies thus have carried out product innovation without any preceding or concomitant process innovation. Slightly larger companies, which principally supply to grocery superstores, however, sometimes need to make minor changes in manufacturing to create new products. In these cases, process innovation, if indeed it occurs, is a by-product of product innovation. Because customer tastes have been changing over time and buyers are looking for new kinds of food, there is often discussion between food companies and large retailers about whether a new product to cater to this newly emerging need is possible and potentially profitable. If there is consensus, then the subsequent search for ways and means to produce it sometimes leads to the realisation that current manufacturing methods may have to be altered to produce it. This process change, however, is achieved not by inventing new kinds of machinery or manufacturing methods but by using manufacturing equipment not used previously. The resultant process innovation is thus new to the firm but not new to the industry.

In terms of radical versus incremental innovation, the case study companies engage very much in incremental change. Although they carry out some imitation, new products usually reflect incremental change, which is most often marginal but sometimes quite substantial. New-to-the-firm innovations thus are far more numerous than new-to-the-market ones.

To sum up, the evidence from the case studies suggests that innovation in the case study companies is more technical and less organisational; it is largely in products and less frequently in processes; it is very often incremental and rarely radical; it is mostly new to the firm and less frequently new to the market.

In the results of the survey to triangulate the case study findings, most propositions emerging from the case studies are verified. Confirmation of survey proposition, 'innovative companies' successful new products are very different from their existing products' appear to suggest that case study observation on incremental product innovation is not borne out in the larger Scottish survey involving all 85 companies. However, the fact that this proposition is rejected in the segregated data analysis involving 59 'low-tech' companies, 23 'high-tech' companies, 29 food & drinks companies, 53 non-food & drinks companies, 43 'young' companies, 40 'old' companies and 68 small companies means that the case study finding on incremental innovation is observed in a wide variety of subgroups of innovative Scottish companies. In fact, it is only the subgroup of 15 larger companies, which is not engaged in incremental innovation. As the case study companies are all small and the only subgroup of survey companies that does not show evidence on incremental innovation are larger companies, it appears that only larger companies can afford to engage in costly radical innovation. The rest of the Scottish companies – even in the nonfood sector and even with high technology orientation – like the case study companies, are focussed on incremental innovation.

Determinants of innovation

Following is a reexamination of some of the prominent determinants of innovation discussed in Chapter 2, in the light of the findings of this research detailed in Chapters 7 and 8.

Internal strategic factors

Market orientation

A strong market orientation was found to be the most visible common denominator in the conduct of the investigated businesses. All the case study companies show significant market orientation, as out of 12 possible indicators they demonstrate evidence on an average of eight indicators. We can thus say that innovative Scottish food companies exhibit a high level of market orientation.

The triangulation survey of 85 innovative Scottish companies confirms all propositions taken from the analysis of case study results on market orientation, except one. It rejects *the long span of market experience*. The survey companies are fairly well distributed across age cohorts, with 40 companies in the 10-year-plus age group and 43 in the less-than-10-year age group.[2] The long span of market experience in the case study companies may have been influenced by the way these companies were selected. The search was made for small Scottish food companies known for successful development of new products. The companies that are operating for longer periods are known to more people than are start-ups, and so when inquiries were made for recommending case study companies, the recommended companies turned out to be those that are in the market for longer periods.

Learning processes

The case study companies boast of rich learning and knowledge construction processes both in innovation and in routine manufacturing. For long they have been accumulating and imparting practical trade knowledge to new generation of family members and new employees. An insatiable appetite for new knowledge and a willingness to travel an extra mile to gain it are also quite visible.

The triangulation survey of 85 innovative Scottish companies confirms the proposition on *continuous learning* taken from the analysis of case study results on learning processes.

Technology policy

It is observed that only some elements of a technology policy orientation are visible in the case study companies. Commitment towards innovation, recruitment of technical people, investing funds in the development of new technology, development of new ideas, products and processes all are evident in the conduct of these businesses. These companies, however, do not carry out R&D separately, and their product development process runs concurrent with manufacturing. This confirms that the informal nature of R&D function in these enterprises is similar to what has been previously reported in literature (Kleinknecht, 1987; Santarelli & Sterlacchini, 1990; Kleinknecht & Reijnen, 1991 and Sterlacchini, 1999).

'Absence of formal R&D' was chosen from the analysis of technology policy as an important case study finding to be tested through the triangulation survey. This is confirmed in the tests involving all 85 companies as well as most subgroups of companies in segregated data analysis. In case however, of 23 high-tech companies and 15 larger companies, this proposition is not supported. The intuitive expectation that high-tech and larger companies would carry out formal R&D, is thus confirmed by the survey. This again highlights the point made earlier. The subgroups of companies, which are distinctly different from the case study companies, have aspects of product innovation, not observed in the case study companies.

Cooperation and networks

Out of seven case study companies, all provide evidence on some kind of cooperation and networking with external entities. This cooperation and networking, however, is utilised for the purpose of new product development by only four companies, and only two companies cooperate for new product development with other food companies. The premier role of cooperation and networking amongst same-sector SMEs reported in the literature thus is not observed in significant amounts in the case study companies.

In the triangulation survey, the respondents were asked to choose between customers, suppliers, competitors and Scottish Enterprise as their networking partners, with the option to mark as many as applicable. Of all survey companies, 93% showed customers and 58% showed suppliers as their partners. The survey, however, shows that only 20% of innovative companies cooperate with Scottish Enterprise. The more troubling conclusion here, however, is that only two of 85 survey companies and none of the case study companies are networking with universities for product innovation. In this context, it is pertinent to note that Frenz *et al.* (2004) attribute Scotland's good performance as a novel product and process innovator despite low intramural investment in R&D to 'the Scottish innovators' higher propensity to enter into cooperative arrangements for innovation with the universities and research organisations'. Neither the case studies nor the survey finds any evidence of such behaviour.

Managerial efficiency and financial resources

Beaver & Jennings (2000) believe that the entrepreneur and the key decision makers in the firm must possess a unique and diverse set of managerial skills and capabilities to carry out successful innovation. In the same context, Grieve-Smith & Fleck (1987) point out that small firms have serious problems in obtaining and grooming requisite managerial talent, since they cannot afford the pay and prerequisites the large firms usually provide.

Managerial inadequacies within SMEs such as poor planning and financial judgement also make innovation impossible (Barber *et al.*, 1989). The other indicated managerial deficiencies include insufficient delegation, high turnover of managerial staff (Nooteboom, 1994) and dependence on word-of-mouth sales without any coordinated marketing effort (Oakey, 1991).

None of the above is observed in the case study companies. On the contrary, these organisations exhibit remarkable managerial efficiency. They also demonstrate significant delegation. During the process of new product development, there is involvement of people from a variety of functions, and everybody's opinion is seriously considered. It is a firm conviction in these companies that good ideas and valid objections to them can come from anywhere, and the question of insufficient delegation does not apply to them. As mentioned previously, these businesses are dependent for both new product development and routine management on the ability of a handful of people, which in most cases include the owner entrepreneur. Only a small number of other managers are needed, and no indication is given that there is any difficulty in recruiting or retaining them. Bakers and chefs are the technical people pivotal to food-company innovation, and the case study companies have been able to get and keep high-calibre people in these departments. The reason may be that amongst their kind, these are relatively more successful companies and pay reasonably well. They are also not in direct competition with any big companies for the kind of products that they make and so not susceptible to poaching. Truly creative individuals employed by these enterprises love the charged, challenging and entrepreneurial environment of these enterprises and do not seem willing to go to big bureaucratic businesses for extra money. Marketing inefficiencies, similarly, are not applicable here, as many of these enterprises market their produce through the large retailers, which are involved from the very beginning of product development process. Most of their products are therefore marketed successfully. One case study company, not supplying to grocery superstores, too has a successful and growing export trade. The role of Scottish Enterprise is also vital here as it supports these enterprises in whatever aspect of managerial capability they may be lacking.

Moreover, unlike the high-tech innovation of their counterparts in new technology sectors, innovation by low-tech traditional SMEs does not need considerable financial resources. They are thus able to carry out innovation and new product development without any major financial constraints. There is also no evidence of a paucity of managerial staff. All the case study companies are able to recruit and retain requisite managerial talent. In many cases, the entrepreneurs themselves are adequately skilled and endowed in innovative abilities and do not need much external recruitment. They have also been able to develop their markets well without any major marketing effort or large advertising budgets.

Three main conclusions from the analysis of *managerial efficiency and human and financial resources* are included for testing in the survey.

1   Innovative food companies are able to engage in innovation and new product development without any significant financial constraints.
2   Innovative food companies do not face a shortage of competent people to develop new products.
3   Innovative food companies demonstrate an ability to develop markets without any major advertising or marketing effort.

The survey rejects the first conclusion and confirms the remaining two. These results are repeated across most subgroups of companies in segregated data analysis. Unlike the case study companies, the survey companies, including those from the food and drinks sector, report that they face significant financial constraints in new product development, which obviously means that the case study companies are better endowed than other innovative Scottish companies, a fact highlighted later in this chapter. However, the conclusion that innovative companies do not face a shortage of competent people to develop new products is confirmed by the overall survey results as well as in the segregated testing involving all subgroups except 29 food and drinks companies. On this count the case study companies are similar to other innovative Scottish companies but dissimilar to other innovative Scottish food and drinks companies. As discussed earlier, the reason for this may be that the size distribution of case study companies and that of food and drinks survey companies is significantly different.

Internal nonstrategic determinants

Age and size

In the case study companies, age does not emerge as an influence on the innovation process. On the other hand, as all case study companies are small, the influence of size is not ascertainable.

Schumpeter's analysis on the age and size of enterprise as innovation-influencing variables, from where these factors are drawn as potential determinants of innovation in this research, is based on one premise. To him, creation of new technology permeates all kinds of innovation. In 1932, he sees small new firms creating new technology and causing in its wake creative destruction, and in 1942, he observes large and established firms using their resources to develop new technologies. Schumpeter's view of innovation thus is essentially technology-driven. It does not apply to the case study companies and for that matter to innovation in any low-tech sector. The case study companies do not need to develop new technology to create new goods. They are able to do so using the existing technology. The case studies therefore can neither corroborate nor dispel either of the two Schumpeterian hypotheses. They suggest, though, one of their own. In low-tech industries, innovation is independent of the age of enterprise. Although it is difficult to prove it firmly from a qualitative research effort involving case studies of only seven companies, the triangulation survey supports it quite well.

As stated previously from the case studies, a comment on the influence of size on the innovative ability of an enterprise could not be made, as all the case study companies are small. However, the survey allowed an opportunity to test the influence of size on product innovation. It discovered that the size does matter, and a larger Scottish company is more likely to be innovative than its smaller counterparts.

Innovative workforce

Some analysts claim that success in innovation is people-dependent rather than resource-dependent (Rothwell, 1983, 1992) and it is the nature and quality of its workforce that would determine whether a business is able to innovate or not. In the case study companies, innovation is clearly people-driven. In this low-tech sector, the product development process, not too resource-consuming, depends heavily on the creativity and innovativeness of people in the product development teams. It is also pointed out by the analysts that small businesses cannot match the pay, career prospects and job security provided by large firms, and they are thus unable to compete for skilled labour (Bosworth, 1989), which is a prerequisite for successful innovation, particularly during the initial stage of product development (Adams, 1982). KPMG's survey *Aiming to Grow in 2005* reports that 33% of Scottish SMEs complain that skill shortages have a detrimental impact on their new product development process (SFDF Manifesto, 2007). However, this study finds that obtaining and grooming requisite managerial talent is not an issue with either the case study companies or the survey companies.

The case study finding that creative people play crucial roles in new product development is supported unequivocally by the survey. The proposition that product development teams are made up of creative people is confirmed in the test involving all 85 companies as well as in the tests involving every company subgroup in the segregated data analysis.

Other explanations

The case study companies investigated in this research are both innovative and successful. As discussed in Chapter 2, the literature on business performance has consistently linked business success to innovation. Therefore, a possible conclusion to be drawn here could be that these companies are successful because of their innovation. However, as most businesses do well when the economy is expanding, one possible alternate explanation could be that these companies have succeeded due to expansion in the Scottish economy of which they are a part. To capture the status of growth in Scotland during recent years, the growth trend in the Scottish economy from 1998 to 2012 is shown in Figure 8.2.

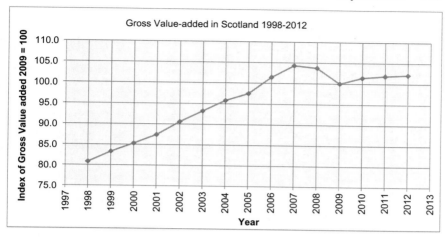

Figure 8.2 Scottish GVA index

Figure 8.2 shows that, barring the period of recent recession (2007–2009), the Scottish economy has been growing continuously. This however, has not been a period of rapid growth. During this period, the Scottish economy grew on an average at 1.7% per annum (Scottish Government, 2013). Even if we consider growth only in the prerecession period, the expansion in Scottish economy between 1998 and 2007 has been 2.9% per annum (Scottish Government, 2013). Against this, the case study companies have done significantly better.

Although data on growth rates of these companies is not specifically collected, the available indirect evidence shows that these are unusually fast growing companies, and the country's rate of growth between 2% to 3% is no comparison. For instance, Company C was expecting its turnover to grow from £5.2 million in 2006 to £7 million in 2007. This converts to a 35% growth in one year. As reported by Company D, its revenue was growing at 20% per annum in 2006. Company E's website mentions that the company doubled its production capacity between 2002 and 2007. This translates into a 40% per annum growth in capacity. Company G grew between 2000 and 2007 at a compound annual rate of 10% per annum. These statistics show that these companies' growth performance is far better than 2% to 3% per annum expansion in the Scottish economy. Their success therefore must have occurred for reasons other than expanding economy and from the findings of this research; innovation appears to be a very strong contender as a contributing factor.

A comparison of these companies' performance with what was happening to the rest of the food and drinks industry in Scotland during 1998–2012 is also worth considering in this context.

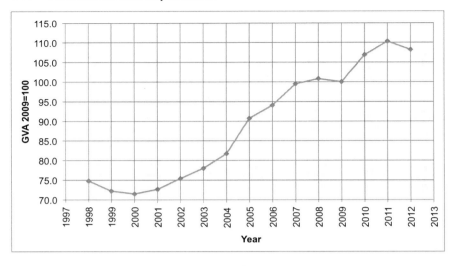

Figure 8.3 Scottish food and drinks GVA index

Figure 8.3 shows that Scottish food and drinks industry grew by 2.7% per annum between 1998 and 2012. This again shows that the performance of these companies was not caused by general economic conditions and they out-performed the Scottish economy as well as the Scottish food and drinks sector.

Summing up: Factors affecting innovation and new product development in Scottish enterprises

The findings from the case studies after their triangulation through a survey of innovative Scottish companies show that innovation and new product development in the Scottish enterprises can be attributed to the following:

1   Strong *market orientation* reflected in their ability to explore and reach potential markets, fit between market needs and the firm's resources, understanding of customer needs and user circumstances and flexibility of their production methods.
2   High calibre *learning processes* reflected in continuous learning.
3   A *technology policy* underscored by an absence of formal R&D.
4   *Cooperation and networking,* principally with customers and suppliers.
5   *Managerial adequacy* reflected in the ability to develop markets without major advertising or marketing efforts and human-resource adequacy confirmed by the availability of competent people to develop new products, but *financial inadequacy* highlighted by financial constraints in new product development.
6   Creativity and innovative proclivity of people involved in the NPD process.

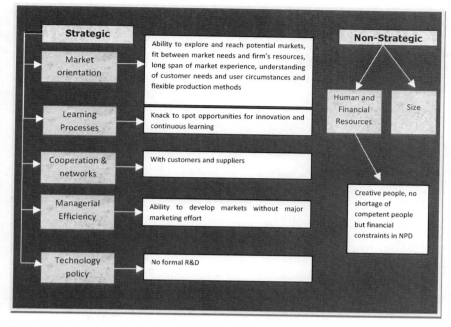

Figure 8.4 Innovation determinants identified in case studies and confirmed by the survey

The underlying process of innovation in the case study companies

The innovation process in the case study companies passes through three distinct stages, involving generation, validation and implementation of new product ideas.

Idea generation is not a problem for these businesses, driven, as they are, by some very creative people. Though the main entrepreneur is the most prolific generator of ideas in these businesses, other individuals, with equally high innovation proclivity, often supplement the idea generation task. There is no evidence of a formal idea generation process and very rarely market research is undertaken to search for new product ideas. Instead, most businesses have a close and regular contact with customers whose constant feedback fuels their creativity.

In some businesses, idea validation is a two-stage process, but in most the validation passes through three stages. In two-stage validation, usually the views of friends, relatives and employees are sought. In the three-stage cases, the idea is first internally validated by a small group of people associated with product development and who being impacted by it, and then it is validated by one or more major customers, usually supermarkets or the up-market grocery chains. Keeping on board those impacted by it from the very beginning helps in understanding and sorting out any teething troubles that may come up when the product is formally commissioned. Companies using a two-stage process are smaller companies serving a niche market, such as organic food or ice cream, and need little changes in existing manufacturing to produce the new product. Idea validation, though largely informal, works well because a large number of people, representing a variety of internal functions (as well as the customer representatives, in the three-stage version) interact continuously, closely, scrutinising the potential products from a host of perspectives. The validation process appears seamless and woven into the daily company routine.

The idea-implementation stage of new product development is very much concurrent and cross-functional, and involves intensive consultation. The customers, which in most cases are grocery superstores, are involved in the implementation process from the outset. The success rate of new products in the case study companies is very high, and they are able to put products in the market in a relatively short period. One of the reasons for such success, despite little or no market research, is that many of these companies do not have to get it right the first time. As the product is a food item, bought in small quantities on a daily basis, the companies continue to monitor customer reactions after the launch and are able to make changes for some time, even as it is being produced, packed and put on the shelves (though some supermarkets do not allow this). Early customer reactions continue to influence product changes until the companies get it right. Despite such a trial-and-error approach, implementation does not take long in case study companies. The process from ideas to final products is completed within a year at the most, and in most cases in less than 6 months.

There is evidence of extensive Scottish Enterprise support to case study companies. The support, however, does not relate to any particular component of the innovation process, such as idea generation, validation or implementation but is rather for a broad spectrum of general business functions, many of them unrelated to innovation. Scottish Enterprise support is targeted towards businesses with growth potential. As the case study companies have obvious growth potential, they have become a natural choice for support, which is comprehensive. It can be said that case study companies are able to focus on innovation, as Scottish Enterprise is extending help to growth (read, innovative) companies for just about every aspect of running the business. These businesses not merely acknowledge this support they also are clearly appreciative of its contribution. Most companies at the time of the interview were either being helped by Scottish Enterprise or were contemplating seeking advice. Scottish Enterprise support, however, is not free or even cheap, and some of the businesses are sceptical about the quality of work done against the costs. The Scottish Enterprise seems to reduce support as an enterprise grows on its own. As one of the respondents interpreted this as waning interest, Scottish Enterprise needs to communicate its approach to the supported businesses more clearly. There is also the feeling that Scottish Enterprise is passing through financial difficulties and has become more bureaucratic, compromising its ability to help.

In the NPD process in the case study companies, product, process, logistics, supply chain and packaging innovations are interwoven. In product innovation, the underlying idea is not merely to be different but also to offer quality that is superior to what is currently available. The approach is to look at the existing offerings, contemplate what they lack and then use the expertise they have to try to create a superior version or versions that suit the British and Scottish tastes. There is very little evidence of radical innovation and some signs of imitation. As these are mostly small-volume-large-variety businesses, they have plenty of scope for incremental change; the predominant theme, therefore, is that of incremental innovation.

Apart from the innate creativity of people at the helm, the exceptional flexibility of these organisations makes them successful innovators. The flexibility comes from being of small size, being labour intensive, from being not too rigid about rules and procedures. Their innovative advantage stems from the fact that the large businesses using automated processes cannot show the agility needed to alter their products quickly to suit changing customer needs as much as these companies can. A combination of factors thus seems to be at work. On the demand side, pressure from the grocery superstores to change the product and packaging driven by changing consumer tastes and preferences and on the supply side the creative urge of some exceptionally gifted people, their long experience in the food industry and the flexibility and speed of their organisations to develop and deliver new goods in quick time.

A major finding of this study is the role of grocery superstores in driving innovation in the case study companies. All investigated businesses, except one, supply mainly to the superstores. Remarkable complementary roles played by small food companies and superstores in steering the food sector innovation in Scotland were observed. The complementariness between the two works something like this. For a small food company the most obvious path to fast growth and assured survival is to become a supplier to superstores. Superstores, however, are reluctant to change their incumbent suppliers, even if they are offered better quality of the same product at a lower price by a new supplier. On the other hand, as the competition in the grocery trade is becoming increasingly variety-based, they are highly receptive to new products and look proactively for innovators. The most obvious choice for a small food company is thus to create new products, if it can, if it wishes to become a multiple's supplier.

This investigation found significant evidence of networking in the case study companies. There is a long tradition of collaboration in the Scottish food and drinks industry, and evidence of its beneficial consequences. Networking, however, is shaped here more by complementariness rather than the need for the competitors to work together for their mutual benefits. These companies network more often with their customers and suppliers and less often with their competitors. There is one distinct type of intrafirm networking in existence. Many of them come together and combine their products to create a larger and more complete menu. They then market this composite menu through one single marketing effort.

In the case study companies, creation of healthy foods is not the most chosen path to innovation. Food companies, from a market perspective, divide their products in two broad categories: those that people buy for their nutritional needs and those that they buy as a treat or indulgence. There is overwhelming consensus within the industry that it is futile to create healthier versions of indulgences. It is believed that trying to make indulgences healthy compromises their taste and jeopardises the very reason for people to buy them. In a related occurrence, some companies who tried to get into the organic food bandwagon early on subsequently gave up the effort, considering it a mistake, particularly as the bulk of their sale is within Scotland, where healthy living, at least now, is not very popular. Superstores, responsible for driving innovation in this sector, also discourage the creation of healthier versions of indulgences, as they are poor sellers.

Out of seven case study companies, only four are exporting and only one is earning significantly from exports. Some of them do not export because they think they have a big enough market in the UK to cater. For others, willing but unable to export, two factors seem to operate as inhibitors. One, their products are perishable, and two, theirs is a low-volume-high-variety operation. Some of these varieties have export potential, but they sell in such small quantities in a given country that trying to export them makes no economic sense. Only one case study company, which interestingly is also the only one not selling to superstores, has significant revenue coming from US exports, in which it visualises substantial growth potential. This has one interesting implication. Superstores, which are driving innovation in this sector, are also reducing incentives to innovative companies to export. For small companies exporting and selling through grocery superstores, both are plausible routes to rapid growth. Developing an export market, however, is not easy. In contrast, for an innovative food company, getting into the superstores' fold is relatively easy due to high receptivity of superstores to new products.

Another distinguishing feature of the innovation process in food companies in Scotland is the quality of their products. The successful innovative food companies in Scotland not merely develop new products, they develop high-quality new products. For them quality is a prerequisite for innovation. These companies intentionally search for more luxuriant and higher quality products capable of being positioned at the higher end of the value chain. This allows them to charge a premium, making innovation rewarding and profitable. Charging premium, however, is not possible through ordinary products, and so genuine high quality becomes an integral part of product development strategy. At the same time, as the Scottish people in general are not known for being very conscious of the health effects of diet, this bias for quality does not take direction of organic or functional foods but turns more often towards indulgences which fits well with the high-price, high-margin, low-volume models of these businesses.

In the survey conducted to triangulate the findings of case studies, most components of the previously described innovation process observed in the case study companies are reported. Some others, however, are specific to the case study companies and are not seen amongst the survey companies. The survey companies, like the case study companies, use informal methods, and creative individuals play central roles in their product development process. Use of flexible production methods is another component of the innovation process that is reported by the survey companies. Although incremental innovation is not established by the larger survey, its presence is confirmed in a very large number of subgroups of innovative Scottish companies. Close cooperation with customers is observed in the survey companies as well, though unlike the case study companies, their main customers are not large retailers. Innovation in survey companies is very much informal and cross-functional, as it is in the case study companies. The single most important difference between the survey companies and the case study companies is an absence of a complementary role played by large retailers in new product development. As survey companies do not sell their new products through large retailers, absence of this practice amongst them, however, is only expected.

Implications of this research for noninnovative food companies

The innovation process in the investigated companies, as identified in the case studies and confirmed by the survey, is influenced by the initiative, commitment and skills of certain creative individuals. The obvious and relevant question therefore is this: Can other currently noninnovative organisations start and continue a new product development process in absence of such individuals? This research suggests that the noninnovative small food companies may be able to embark on innovation by taking the following route.

As detailed earlier, in some of the case studies companies, the hired employees who possess high innovative proclivity and who have long experience in the food industry play crucial roles. These people are also empowered with sufficient flexibility and discretion in decisions concerning innovation. Implication of this is obvious. Noninnovative organisations willing to embark on a path to innovation should first recruit such people and delegate requisite independence and discretion to them. In two of the case study companies, the hired individuals who have significant authority in product development drive innovation almost single-handedly. It thus seems plausible that if an organisation is able to recruit and empower people with such attributes, they should be able to ignite the innovation process.

The successful new products that have come out of the case study companies are often a variant of their existing products. In the triangulation survey, barring the single subgroup of companies employing more than 50 people, the segregated data analysis of all other subgroups of survey companies support this. The innovation aspirants therefore should proactively search for the answer to the following question: In which way could the products in their hands can be marginally moulded to cater to a long unfulfilled or newly emerging need (Vyas, 2009)? A valuable insight here is that creation of more luxuriant versions or premiumisation of exiting products is the most promising way forward. This allows the product to move up the value chain, the company to charge a better margin and so to quickly recoup the development costs. It also fits well with the high-variety-low-volume manufacturing environment of the small food companies.

After identifying the product idea, the company should validate it through intensive consultation involving all internal and external stakeholders to check for production feasibility as well as market potential. Case studies show that making several variants of a product and offering to let people you know taste them is the simplest and most effective method to ascertain market potential of a new food product.

Improving the product when the product has been put in the market and achieving a good fit between the product and customers' needs requires a high sensitivity and responsiveness to customer reactions during the implementation stage.

Implications of this research for the Government of Scotland

As explained in Chapter 5, there is a need for Scottish Government to rethink its innovation strategy. Its concern and determination to make Scotland a more innovative region are well founded. However, the present strategy to achieve this, based on the presumption that innovation in Scotland is science-led, occurs principally in its high-tech sectors and is caused by investments in R&D, is flawed. It is true that in some businesses innovation does occur in this manner, but such businesses are in a minuscule minority in the Scottish economy. None of the case study companies and, barring the obvious exceptions of high-tech and larger Scottish companies, none of the subgroups of innovative survey companies invest in formal R&D. If the Scottish Government modifies its vision of innovation and focuses its resources on understanding and supporting innovation in its low-tech traditional industries, it can make Scotland a more innovative and competitive region than it is today.

Notes

1 These are preinvention, invention, technical innovation, organisational innovation and innovation beneficiaries.
2 The age of two companies is not known.

References

Adams, A (1982) Barriers to product innovation in small firms: Policy implications, *European Small Business Journal*, 1(1):67–86

Barber, J, Metcalfe, J and Porteous, M (1989) Barriers to growth: The ACARD study, in Barber, J, Metcalfe, J and Porteous, M (Eds) *Barriers to Growth in Small Firms*, London: Routledge

Beaver, G and Jennings, L (2000) Small business, entrepreneurship and enterprise development, *Journal of Strategic Change*, 9(7):397–405

Bosworth, D (1989) Barriers to growth: The labour market, in Barber, J, Metcalfe, J and Porteous, M (Eds) *Barriers to Growth in Small Firms*, London: Routledge

Brenner, Reuven (1990) *Rivalry: In Business, Science, Among Nations*, Cambridge: Cambridge University Press

Dosi, Giovanni (1988) Sources, procedures and microeconomic effects of innovation, *Journal of Economic Literature*, 26(3):1120–71

Edquist, Charles (2001) *The systems of innovation approach and innovation policy: an account of the state of the art*, Lead paper at the DRUID Conference, Aalborg, June 12–15

European Commission (1995) *The Green Paper on Innovation Commission of the European Communities*, Luxembourg: Commission of the European Communities

Frenz, Marion and Oughton, Christine (2005) *Innovation in the UK regions and devolved administrations: a review of the literature*, Final Report for the Department of Trade and Industry and the Office of the Deputy Prime Minister

Frenz, Marion, Michie, Jonathan and Oughton, Christine (2004) *Cooperation and innovation: Evidence from the community innovation survey*, Unpublished paper

Grieve-Smith, A and Fleck, V (1987) Business strategies in small high technology companies, *Long Range Planning*, 20(2):61–8

Grunert, K G, Brunso, K and Soren, B (1997) Food-related lifestyle: Development of a cross-culturally valid instrument for market surveillance, in Kahle, L and Chiagouris, C (Eds) *Values, Lifestyles, and Psychographics*, Mahwah, NJ: Erlbaum, 337–54

Kleinknecht, A and Reijnen, J O N (1991) More evidence on the undercounting of small firm R&D, *Research Policy*, 20(6):579–87

Kleinknecht, A (1987) Measuring R&D in small firms: How much are we missing, *Journal of Industrial Economics*, 36(2):253–56

Le Bars, A, Mangematin, V and Nesta, L (1998) *Innovation in SMEs: The missing link*, Paper presented at the High Technology Small Firms Conference, University of Twente, Enschede

Nooteboom, B (1994) Innovation and diffusion in small firms: Theory and evidence, *Small Business Economics*, 6(5):327–47

Oakey, R (1991) Innovation and the management of marketing in high technology small firms, *Journal of Marketing Management*, 7(4):343–56

OECD (1981) *The Measurement of Scientific and Technical Activities: Proposed Standard Practice for Surveys of Research and Experimental Development*, Paris: OECD

OECD (1997) *The Oslo Manual: Proposed Guidelines for Collecting and Interpreting Technology Innovation Data*, Paris: OECD

Rothwell, R (1983) Innovation and firm size: A case for dynamic complementarily– or is small really beautiful? *Journal of General Management*, 8(3):5–25

Rothwell, R (1992) Successful Industrial Innovation: Critical success factors for the 1990s, *R&D Management*, 22(3):221–39

Santarelli, E and Sterlacchini, A (1990) Innovation, formal vs informal R&D, and firm size: Some evidence from Italian manufacturing firms, *Small Business Economics*, 2(3):223–28

Schumpeter, Joseph A (1934) *The Theory of Economic Development*, Cambridge, MA: Harvard University Press

Schumpeter, Joseph A (1942) *Capitalism, Socialism and Democracy*, New York: Harper & Row

Scottish Government (2013) *Scottish Economic Statistics*, Edinburgh: Scottish Government

SFDF Manifesto (2007) Scottish Food and Drinks federation, www.sfdForGuk/sfdf/SFDF_manifesto_12pp_v8.pdf, accessed 25 September 2007

Sterlacchini, Alessandro (1999) Do innovative activities matter to small firms in non-R&D-intensive industries? An application to export performance, *Research Policy*, 28(8):819–32

Vyas, Vijay (2009) Survival and growth of high-tech SMEs: Some uncommon strategies, in Manimala et al. (Eds) *Enterprise Support Systems: An International Perspective*, New Delhi: Sage

West, M A and Farr, J L (Eds) (1990) *Innovation and Creativity at Work*, Chichester: Wiley

9 Research findings and extant literature

Congruence, conflict and implications

In the final chapter of this book, the last 4 decades of research on innovation in the food and drinks industry presented in Chapter 1 is revisited in the light of the findings of this research.

This research shows that small food companies do not need formal R&D to develop new products. This case study observation is confirmed in all survey subgroups except for larger and high-tech enterprises. This has resonance with evidence in the literature. For instance, Jones (1995), in a cross-country comparison, Galizzi & Venturini (1996) for USA, Ilori *et al.* (2000) for Nigeria and Capitanio *et al.* (2009) for Italy report *low R&D intensity* in the innovative food firms. It is noteworthy here that they do not report *zero* incidence of R&D but only its low intensity. The reason for this variation is that the cited studies include firms of all sizes whereas findings in this book relate only to small companies. This issue is explored in more detail later in the light of some further-related evidence from literature.

The other finding echoed in the literature involves incremental nature of food sector innovation. Koku's (1998) content analysis of news product announcement in the Wall Street Journal, Ernst & Young's (1999) report on new products introduced in the Spanish food industry, Martinez & Briz's (2000) survey of Spanish food companies, Bogue & Ritson's (2006) analysis of new Irish food products and Bhaskaran's (2006) survey of Australian seafood SMEs, all conclude that food industry innovation is singularly incremental. The analysis here, however, goes beyond identifying the incremental nature of innovation in this industry. The fresh insight here is that the direction of this incremental change is towards the development of luxuriant and expensive versions of existing products, or 'premiumisation'. This research also discovers a rationale for this product development emphasis. All case study companies, as well as a large proportion of survey companies, operate within a high-variety-low-volume manufacturing environment. Their newly developed products would sell only in small quantities. They, therefore, must command a premium to recoup the developmental costs. This research, thus, goes beyond 'what happens' and answers 'why it happens' (Whetten, 1989), a question not answered in the previous research.

The literature, however, shows that spurning R&D and being satisfied with only an incremental change is not the behaviour of the very largest of food and drinks corporations. Large multi-national corporations (MNCs) in this sector do not seem to worry too much about the high costs of avant-garde science and are willing to invest in search for drastic new products. Very critically, however, the evidence from the literature also indicates that they do not succeed consistently in this pursuit and successful amongst them are few. Alfranca *et al.* (2004), from an analysis of patents granted in the US between 1977 and 1994 to the largest food and drinks MNCs in the world, find that for any one MNC, an innovative spell lasting more than 4 years is a rare event, and a small number of persistent patentees obtain almost 80% of the all patents granted to food corporations. From this it is obvious that even the most cash-rich food companies in their search for radical new food products fail more often than they succeed. For smaller food companies, it therefore makes good sense to avoid R&D investments and confine them to a non-R&D incremental innovation, which as this research shows they are able to undertake with significant success.

The rationale for this focus on incremental innovation, evasion of apparently 'unnecessary' R&D investments and poor research intensity in the food and drinks sector reported by the researchers is consistent with analysis of findings reported in this book. The previous researchers attribute it to the unchanging nature of consumers' food habits. The literature reveals that historically as well as currently, food consumption is marked by significant conservatism. People generally are unwilling to eat products regularly which are very different from what they usually eat. New product developers, thus, are confronted by a formidable challenge if they wish to develop a radical new food product. Consistent with the findings of this research, Nystrom & Edvardsson (1982) report that consumers' reluctance to try radical new products means that only the food companies developing new products which are variation of their current products achieve NPD success. Galizzi & Venturini (1996), too, find that food consumers in general are unadventurous in their food choices and find it difficult to accept completely new food products. One of their related findings is a lack of strong relationship between R&D intensity and innovation in the food industry. This book, however, reports that this lack of relationship between R&D and innovation is much more pervasive and not confined to the food industry. Barring a small number of high-tech companies and larger companies, all subsections of survey companies as well as all case study companies report that formal R&D has no role in their product development process. Analysing this in combination with Nystrom & Edvardsson's (1982) conclusion stated previously generates a valuable insight. The possibility that significant commercial success can be achieved through incremental innovation without any R&D investments, along with the fact that R&D, in any case, does not guarantee innovation, explains the historical as well as the present dependence on incremental innovation and evasion of R&D investments by small firms in this industry. Although food SMEs continue to engage in innovative activities (Baregheh *et al.*, 2012) the nature of their engagement with innovation has not changed, neither is it likely to change any time soon.

The finding of this research on avoiding the development of healthy foods by small food companies, based on the observation of all but one case study company, is echoed in the study by Bogue & Ritson (2006). They explain that the unexpected failure of low-fat variants to deliver the promised premiums to their creators is caused by food consumers' conservative and resolute attitude, also discussed previously, resulting in the battle between the hedonic value and the perceived health benefits, going in favour of the former. The 'premiumisation' focus of innovative food companies proposed here, together with the inability of newly developed health foods to deliver the premiums as reported by Bogue & Ritson (2006), explains why innovative small Scottish food companies have avoided developing healthy food products. Interestingly, the industry experts continue to maintain that development of low-fat foods promise significant potential in years to come (Longman, 2001). However, neither the finding of this work nor the research anywhere else on the subject so far suggests that the small food companies, as a general trend, are anywhere near realising this.

Another finding relevant here is significant retailer involvement in new product development in the food industry. It is observed in all but one of the case study companies. This has been reported in the literature as well. For instance, Hughes (1997) for UK; Stewart-Knox & Mitchell (2003) for USA, UK and Denmark; Fortuin & Omta (2009) for the Netherlands; Spiekermann (2009) for Germany and Colurcio *et al.* (2012) for Italy and Switzerland report the same. Hingley & Hollingsworth (2003), however, clarify that retailer's interest in encouraging and abetting small food companies to develop new food products is generally focused on creating products for the high end of the value chain, and their objective in this, is to compete with major food brands. When we juxtapose this with the finding reported in this book, that small food companies develop premium products due to their high-variety-low-volume operations, it complements the extant literature and reveals that the two partners in the process collaborate with each other for entirely different reasons. One finding in the literature not resonating with the general tone of our findings is an element of coercion in this relationship reported by van der Valk & Wynstra (2005). They claim that large retailers practically force food companies to either innovate or loose shelf space to a competitor. None of our case study companies that supply to large retailers has reported such coercion. The reason of these contrasting findings, we believe, is that when van der Valk & Wynstra (2005:682) say "either innovate, or loose shelf space to the competitor", it is obviously a comment towards a company with the shelf space that has failed to innovate. The case study companies, in contrast, have a good record of innovation. In fact, most of them entered the supermarket shelves by the sheer fact that they offered an innovative product. Another finding reported in literature but subsumed in our findings only implicitly is that when a small food company networks with a large retailer with conflicting goals, the resultant conflict helps them maintain 'the competitive driving force and creativity' (Colurcio *et al.*, 2012).

The finding involving cross-functional cooperation within the enterprise is consistent with the food innovation literature. It is reported by Suwannaporn & Speece (2000) in a study of 17 large companies as well as that of 114 medium to large companies (Suwannaporn & Speece, 2003), and of 93 companies, nearly half of which are SMEs (Dhamvithee *et al.*, 2005). This size distribution of investigated companies in the literature gives an indication that the role of cross-functional cooperation in new product innovation success cuts across firm size. The presence of Taiwanese firms in the first cited study and a similar finding by Capitanio *et al.* (2009) in a study of 234 Italian firms suggest some validity to these findings across regions.

Findings in the literature on innovative food company's ability to respond quickly to changing customer tastes (Bogue, 2001), involvement of top management in product development (Ilori *et al.*, 2000), the quality of human capital (Fortuin & Omta, 2009), flexibility and emphasis on product quality (Bogue, 2001) and market and consumer knowledge (Stewart-Knox & Mitchell, 2003) are consistent with conclusions of this book. However, outsourcing of activities (Spaulding & Woods, 2006), export orientation (Karantininis *et al.*, 2010) and regional networking (Gellynck *et al.*, 2007 and Karantininis *et al.*, 2010) was observed in only one case study company each, and was thus not attempted to be investigated in this study.

References

Alfranca, Oscar, Rama, Ruth and Tunzelmann, Nicholas von (2004) Innovation spells in the multinational agri-food sector, *Technovation*, 13(6):343–73

Baregheh, Anahita, Rowley, Jennifer, Sambrook, Sally and Davies, Daffyd (2012) Innovation in food sector SMEs, *Journal of Small Business and Enterprise Development*, 19(2):300–21

Bhaskaran, Suku (2006) Incremental innovation and business performance: Small and medium-size food enterprises in a concentrated industry environment, *Journal of Small Business Management*, 44(1):64–80

Bogue, Joe (2001) New product development and the Irish food sector: A qualitative study of activities and processes, *Irish Journal of Management*, 22(1):171–91

Bogue, Joe and Ritson, Christopher (2006) Integrating consumer information with the new product development process: The development of lighter dairy products, *International Journal of Consumer Studies*, 30(1):44–54

Capitanio, Fabian, Coppola, Adele and Pascucci, Stefano (2009) Indications for drivers of innovation in the food sector, *British Food Journal*, 111(8):820–38

Colurcio, Maria, Wolf, Patricia, Kocher, Pierre-Yves and Russo Spena, Tiziana Russo (2012) Asymmetric relationships in networked food innovation processes, *British Food Journal*, 114(5):702–27

Dhamvithee, Pisit, Shankar, Bhavani, Jangchud, Anuvat and Wuttijumnong, Phaisarn (2005) New product development in Thai agro-industry: Explaining the rates of innovation and success in innovation, *International Food and Agribusiness Management Review*, 8(3):1–17

Ernst & Young (1999) *New Product Introduction, Successful Innovation/Failure: A Fragile Boundary*, Paris: Ernst & Young

Fortuin, Frances T J M and Omta, S W F (2009) Innovation drivers and barriers in food processing, *British Food Journal*, 111(8):839–51

Galizzi, G and Venturini, L (1996) *Economics of Innovation: The Case of Food Industry*, Heidelberg: Physica-Verlag

Gellynck, X, Vermeire, B and Viaene, J (2007) Innovation in food firms: Contribution of regional networks within the international business context, *Entrepreneurship & Regional Development*, 19(3):209–26

Hingley, M, & Hollingsworth, A (2003) *Competitiveness and power relationships: Where now for the UK food supply chain?* Proceedings, the 19th Annual IMP Conference, Lugano, Switzerland

Hughes, Alex (1997) The changing organization of new product development for retailers' private labels: A UK-US comparison, *Agribusiness*, 13(2):169–84

Ilori, M O, Oke, J S and Sanni, S A (2000) Management of new product development in selected food companies in Nigeria, *Technovation*, 20(6):333–42

Jones, Peter (1995) Developing new products and services in-flight catering, *International Journal of Contemporary Hospitality Management*, 7(2):24–28

Karantininis, K, Sauer, J and Furtan, W H (2010) Innovation and integration in the agri-food industry, *Food Policy*, 35(2):112–12

Koku, Paul Sergius (1998) Innovation and information management in the food industry, *British Food Journal*, 100(6):278–85

Longman, B (2001) *Future Innovations in Food 2001: Forward-Focused NPD and Maximizing Brand Value*, London: Reuters Business Insight

Martinez, Garcia Marian and Briz, Julian (2000) Innovation in the Spanish food and drinks industry, *International Food and Agribusiness Management Review* 3(2):155–76

Nystrom, Harry and Edvardsson, Bo (1982) Product innovation in food processing– A Swedish survey, *R&D Management*, 12(2):67–72

Spaulding, Aslihan D and Woods, Timothy A (2006) An analysis of the relationship between supply-chain management practices and new product development time: A case of the North American confectionery manufacturers, *Journal of Food Distribution Research*, 37(2):1–11

Spiekermann, Uwe (2009) Twentieth-century product innovations in the German food industry, *Business History Review*, 83(2):291–315

Stewart-Knox, Barbara and Mitchell, Peter (2003) What separates the winners from the losers in new food product development? *Trends in Food Science & Technology*, 14(1):58–64

Suwannaporn, Prisana and Speece, Mark (2000) Continuous learning process in new product development in the Thai food-processing industry, *British Food Journal*, 102(8):598–614

Suwannaporn, Prisana and Speece, Mark (2003) Marketing research and new product development success in Thai food processing, *Agribusiness*, 19(2):169–88

van der Valk, Wendy and Wynstra, Finn (2005) Supplier involvement in new product development in the food industry, *Industrial Marketing Management*, 34(7): 681–694

Whetten, David A (1989) What constitutes a theoretical contribution? *Academy of Management Review*, 14(4):490–95

Index